Corporate Governance and the Timeliness of Change

Corporate Governance and the Timeliness of Change

Reorientation in 100 American Firms

HUGH SHERMAN
AND
RAJESWARARAO CHAGANTI

QUORUM BOOKS
Westport, Connecticut • London

Library of Congress Cataloging-in-Publication Data

Sherman, Hugh.
    Corporate governance and the timeliness of change : reorientation
in 100 American firms / by Hugh Sherman and Rajeswararao Chaganti.
        p.   cm.
    Includes bibliographical references and index.
    ISBN 1–56720–087–7 (alk. paper)
    1. Organizational change—United States—Longitudinal studies.
    2. Corporate governance—United States—Longitudinal studies.
    I. Chaganti, Rajeswararao.   II. Title.
    HD58.8.S486   1998
    658.4′06—DC21   98–4930

British Library Cataloguing in Publication Data is available.

Library of Congress Catalog Card Number: 98–4930
ISBN: 1–56720–087–7

First published in 1998

Quorum Books, 88 Post Road West, Westport, CT 06881
An imprint of Greenwood Publishing Group Inc.

Printed in the United States of America

The paper used in this book complies with the
Permanent Paper Standard issued by the National
Information Standards Organization (Z39.48–1984).

10 9 8 7 6 5 4 3 2 1

To my wife and son, who have filled my life
with love and happiness.
—H.S.

Contents

Introduction: The New Competitive Landscape

A noted expert on the future, Alvin Toffler (1990), predicted that "fast" firms will be the most successful competitors. Richard D'Aveni, in his book *Hypercompetition: Managing the Dynamics of Strategic Maneuvering* has observed:

> While cost and quality, timing and know-how, strongholds, and deep pockets always played a role in competition, the difference today is the speed and aggressiveness of interaction in these arenas. ... It is not just fast-moving, high-tech industries, such as industries shaken by deregulation, that are facing this aggressive competition. There is evidence that competition is heating up across the board, even in what once seemed to be the most sedate industries. ... Competition on timing and know-how has intensified. (1994, 2)

Business analysts will likely come to view the period of 1980 through 1995 as a turning point in the history of American enterprise. The days when firms could develop a competitive advantage that they could then maintain for years are long gone. Today, companies must actively disrupt their own competitive advantage and the advantages of their competitors. The ability to implement fast-paced change is key to a firm's future success. Firms that are able to initiate and complete change in a relatively short period of time will tend to outperform their rivals.

Before the 1980s, America's largest corporations rarely undertook massive change, and only then when the organization faced a life-threatening crisis. However, in recent years, corporations have been initiating change quickly, and in some cases continuously. This book focuses on a specific type of change event, one that represents massive change, or reorientation. Reorientation is defined as having occurred when a firm changes its corporate structure, corporate-wide control systems, and corporate strategy, all within a two-year period of time. AlliedSignal and Compaq Computers are two case examples reviewed in detail in this book in which a firm has initiated two reorientations in less than seven years. Both firms reoriented the second time despite enjoying superior performance in their respective industries.

We set out to answer the question of why some corporations were able to initiate reorientations relatively quickly while others took years before they responded. For example, Henry Schacht, chief executive officer of Cummins Engine, initiated a reorientation in 1984, a year in which the firm held a commanding 60 percent share of the North American market and achieved a stunning 32 percent return on equity for its shareholders. However, other firms, such as Tenneco, did not initiate a reorientation even though their financial performance continued to be very poor through the entire decade of the 1980s. It was only in 1991, when Tenneco faced a financial crisis and the incumbent chief executive officer was being charged with highly questionable accounting practices, that the board of directors finally responded by appointing a new chief executive officer. In most of the cases we examined, the corporate governance system failed to respond to the need for reorienting the company. Many incumbent executives not only responded slowly to poor financial performance, they often failed to respond at all and were unable to implement a fundamental change in their firm's strategies and practices. It is at these times that a firm's board of directors or major shareholders must intervene and force the incumbent management to initiate major change.

In too many cases, a long-tenured chief executive officer has been able to gain control over the board of directors because he or she is also the chair of the board. This allows the chief executive officer to nominate new board members who will be loyal and control board members' access to information. Such boards are unable to properly perform their oversight function.

A CHANGING CORPORATE GOVERNANCE SYSTEM

Late in the 1980s, it became apparent that a fundamental shift in the power relationship between a firm's shareholders and its professional managers was taking place. Shareholders increased their control over the firm's professional managers, demanding that managers respond more quickly to poor financial performance and to changes in the competitive environment.

Stockholders were becoming increasingly dissatisfied with management's slowness and the ineffectiveness of their actions in trying to adapt to new environmental conditions. Many stockholders became convinced that management did not keep the shareholders' interests in mind while developing and implementing new strategies.

Numerous stories have appeared in the business press chronicling the efforts of shareholders to exert control over corporate management. *Fortune* magazine's January 11, 1993, issue featured a cover story by T. Stewart titled "The King Is Dead," proclaiming the death of the imperial corporate presidency. An increasing number of chief executive officers have been forced to relinquish control of their organizations to others who will more quickly implement massive corporate change.

Large shareholders, including, most importantly, institutional investors, were pressing their firms' managers to put shareholder value above their own objectives. Executives have fought back by developing formal safeguards to prevent shareholders (including corporate raiders) from taking away their decision-making control. These safeguards have included "poison pills," "greenmail," and the establishment of employee stock ownership programs. A poison pill gives shareholders the right to purchase additional stock in the company or the acquirer's company at a discounted price once the would-be acquirer has accumulated a certain number of shares. Since the built-in discount can be as high as 50 percent, all of the firm's existing shareholders have a monetary incentive to participate. The acquirer's shareholders cannot participate and will see their own equity interest become worth less.

From the existing shareholder's perspective, greenmail is perhaps the most unacceptable approach to avoiding a takeover attempt. Management makes an agreement to buy out the would-be acquirer at a price substantially above the current market price, if the would-be purchaser drops their takeover attempt. The would-be acquirer makes a huge profit without having to purchase the company.

In one case reviewed in this book (Phillips Petroleum), entrenched management sold off valuable oil properties, paid greenmail to corporate raiders, and established an employee stock ownership plan (ESOP) in a successful fight to prevent two back-to-back takeover attempts.

Although in many corporations the battle for control may still be in progress, other corporate managers have learned their lessons from the experiences of the 1980s and 1990s. More and more executive teams are becoming responsive to shareholder interests, which often requires the speedy initiation of reorientations in an attempt to improve financial performance.

DESCRIPTION OF THE RESEARCH STUDY

The study reported in this book examines data collected from 100 manufacturing corporations drawn from twenty-two industries in the United States. Fifty-three of the firms were from volatile industries, while forty-seven firms were from relatively stable industries. A complete list of the corporations that were examined and the methodology that was used to select the sample are included in Appendix B.

Each corporation in the study was tracked for nine years, from 1983 to 1991. For a selected sample of these firms, we examined the firm's subsequent behavior and financial success from 1992 to 1996. The complete database is quite sizable. It includes stock analysts' reports, competitive strategies, annual reports, descriptions of corporate structure and control systems, institutional owner characteristics, characteristics of top management team members and corporate board members, chief executives' backgrounds, and the performance history of the firms.

The best way to understand the complex change process, including the speed at which reorientation is initiated and the firm's subsequent performance, is by reviewing actual examples in detail. The forces that trigger a reorientation are extremely complex and dynamic, so it is important to understand the context within which a firm is operating. Therefore, from the pool of 100 firms, we have selected nine companies, which we explain in detail so that the forces that caused change to be initiated can be more clearly understood. For each case we give a brief background of the industry, the company, and the critical events that led up to the initiation of the reorientation. We also describe what happened to the firms after the reorientation was completed in order to identify which change processes led to the most sucessful subsequent performance.

PLAN OF THE BOOK

This book is divided into five chapters and three technical appendixes. Chapter 1 discusses the characteristics of major corporate change, reviewing the major models that describe organizational change. Chapters 2 through 4 discuss the mechanisms that trigger a firm to undertake reorientation and represent the key findings of this study. Chapter 2 explains the role of the firm's prior financial performance in setting the context within which a reorientation occurs. The role of the chief executive officer and the top management team in initiating a reorientation is discussed in Chapter 3. In Chapter 4, we review the role of large shareholders, institutional investors, and members of the board of directors.

Chapter 5 discusses our conclusions concerning how firms can implement reorientations in a more timely and effective manner. Appendix A provides summary statistical tables. Appendix B provides a detailed discussion of the research methodology that was used in this study. Included in this section is a description of the sample of firms, the approach used to gather data and to identify reorientations, and the statistical techniques that were used to analyze the data.

Finally, Appendix C reviews the corporate governance and strategic change literature.

Corporate Governance and the Timeliness of Change

1

Characteristics and Models of Change

The purpose of this chapter is to provide a description of the theoretical framework that was used as a basis for conducting the research reported in this book. It is important to understand the characteristics associated with organizational change, including the depth, pervasiveness, and timeliness. It is also useful to review the major models that have been used in the business literature to describe change. This will make it clear why we believe that the punctuated equilibrium model offers the most accurate description of massive organizational change and why it serves as the framework that is the basis of our research.

The depth of change refers to the extent to which the change involves a shift in the strategic orientation of a firm. This change has been categorized into first-order and second-order change. Most organizational change is first-order change because it involves adjustments to the firm's existing strategies and organizational practices. Second-order change is considerably more extensive, and therefore less common. It must include the following three characteristics. First, core processes of the firm, such as the organizational structure or the management decision-making processes, are altered. Second, the culture of the organization is changed; this includes the beliefs, norms of behavior, and organizational heroes. Third, the firm's corporate strategy and mission are changed (Levy 1986).

The second characteristic associated with change involves how pervasive it is or how many organizational elements change. If the strategic orientation of the firm is to be altered, then the change must be pervasive. The more pervasive the change is for large corporations, the longer it normally takes to successfully implement that change. To initiate pervasive change takes years because it requires many different change agents or champions. Often this kind of change requires an outstanding, driven leader, such as Jack Welch of General Electric. Welch set the wheels of change in motion, created the vision of where the organization needed to go, and motivated thousands of employees to implement the change as he intended.

The third characteristic is the timeliness of change. Today, corporate managers are more concerned than ever before with managing the process by which firms adapt their organizational competencies to meet the threats and opportunities created by environmental change. Many management concepts, such as process, adaptation, and change, are time-based concepts. Organizations have a finite period of time within which to adapt if they are to survive. An increasing number of chief executive officers has been forced to relinquish control of their organizations to others who will more quickly implement massive corporate change. In today's competitive environment, time has become one of the most important determinants of firm performance.

This book is concerned with the firm's ability to enact reorientation in a timely manner, which represents second-order change that is pervasive.

THEORETICAL MODELS OF CHANGE

Contemporary organizational theory has two main opposing perspectives regarding organizational change. These perspectives are the adaptive view (whereby managers are able to implement change) versus the inertial view (whereby organizations are not able to adapt to environmental change). One important theory that attempts to reconcile these different perspectives is the punctuated equilibrium model of change, which is discussed in this chapter. This model was used as the basis for the research conducted for this book (see Table 1.1).

Inertial View

The inertial view describes organizational action as being determined by forces outside the organization. One theory that falls in this area is the population ecology perspective, an approach that applies theories of biological evolution to organizations.

When organizations are founded, managers choose a strategic orientation, such as specialization in a certain market niche or adoption of a broader approach for selling to the market. As a result of environmental conditions, such as industry demand, and competitive conditions, a certain set of critical success factors must be part of the firm's strategic ori-

Table 1.1
Review of Major Change Models

CHARACTERISTICS OF STRATEGIC CHANGE			
THEORY	TIMELINESS	FREQUENCY	MAGNITUDE
A. Inertia theories	untimely	seldom, if ever	small, if any
B. Adaptive theories	moderate to fast	periodic	major
C. Punctuated equilibrium (two periods): Convergence period Revolutionary period	slow fast during short periods of change	infrequent infrequent	minor adjustments major adjustments

entation; otherwise, it will fail. Once this orientation has been chosen, the firm and its managers become subject to strong internal and external pressures that force them to maintain their existing strategic orientation (Hannan and Freeman 1984). For example, the firm will make commitments to a bank in return for loans and to its own employees in return for their agreement to come to work for the firm. These resource providers will not allow the organization to make major changes to its strategic orientation.

If these environmental conditions remain the same over time, then one type of firm (with the appropriate strategic orientation) will eventually emerge as the sole survivor. This firm will fit the needs created by that environment. The population ecology model is the most extreme view of organizations because it depicts firm executives as having little ability to make any changes to the behavior of their firms.

The inertial view, as expressed by theories such as population ecology, suggests that organizations will not change or will change only infrequently and in small, incremental steps. This view implies that organizations are inflexible and unable to respond in a timely manner to environmental opportunities and threats.

Michael Porter's (1980) work is consistent with the inertial view of organizations. Porter's model is one of the most important and popular theoretical models in use today. He contends that the characteristics of the industry in which a firm competes will be the major determinant of its financial performance. Porter has identified five key industry characteristics, or forces, that affect firms: the degree and type of rivalry, the power of the buyers, the power of suppliers, the threat of new entrants into the industry, and the availability of substitute products. Based on the power of these forces and the characteristics of the firm, he identifies three generic strategies that can be used by the firm to survive. The three strategies are cost leadership (lowest cost producer), differentiation (development of a high-quality or innovative product), and a focus strategy (emphasis on exploiting a narrow market segment). Porter suggests that industry or competitive conditions determine which strategy management must choose.

Porter's key argument is that the industry environment dictates the behavior of the firm and determines its subsequent success. The actions of executives have little impact on firm's the financial outcome. His view is not as extreme as that of the population ecologists because in this model, management is seen as able to adapt as industry conditions change. However, this adaptive ability is constrained by the industry characteristics and mobility barriers.

Adaptive View

The adaptive view argues that managers do have the ability to alter their organization's practices to adapt to environmental demands as well as the ability to alter the demands of the environment. Strategy is seen as a comprehensive, forward-looking activity that is directed by top managers.

Alfred Chandler (1962), in a historical review of major U.S. firms, observed that exceptional leadership was often critical for firms to be able to overcome the resistance of their employees. Chandler traced the histories of some seventy large industrial firms, including General Motors, DuPont, Sears, and Standard Oil. He found that as a firm increased the number of different products it produced and as the demands of the environment increased, firms were forced to change their structure. In general, they moved from using functional structures to using divisional structures. In the cases that Chandler investigated, he found that internal and external resistance impeded the adoption of these new divisional structures. Existing managers resisted structural change because they wanted to maintain their current position and power. However, ultimately the firms were able to overcome this resistance and adopt new structures that better matched their new strategies. Often new executives had to join the firm before this resistance could be overcome.

According to this model, the only way firms can accomplish substantial change is to schedule a lengthy, systematic, formal analysis of the environment. During this process, management chooses a comprehensive, integrated strategy. The process is very time-consuming, but once the strategy has been chosen, it is implemented relatively quickly.

Punctuated Equilibrium Model

Both the inertial and the adaptive models have been found to accurately describe firm behavior during different periods of the organization's history. However, neither model is able to adequately describe a firm's behavior during all periods.

We found that the punctuated equilibrium model offers the best description of organizational behavior by reconciling the inertial and adaptive views of organization change. The punctuated equilibrium model recognizes that large organizations are highly resistant to change. For the majority of the time, firms only initiate incremental change, while forces of resistance prevent radical change (Tushman and Romanelli 1985). These forces of resistance include the managers' limited cognitive abilities, which prevent them from fully understanding the environment, and the organization's obligations to stakeholders inside and outside the organization.

Consistent with the adaptive model, the punctuated equilibrium model contends that organizations can implement change. Once in a while, revolutionary change occurs, during which time the firm's strategies, structure, and control systems are significantly altered. Michael Tushman and Elaine Romanelli (1985) define reorientations as "relatively short periods of discontinuous change where strategy, power, structure and controls are fundamentally transformed toward a new coalition" (p. 147).

Executive leadership is the critical change agent in overcoming the internal forces of inertia and adapting the firm's strategic orientation to adjust to the external competitive market forces. The firm's executive team initiates and directs reorientations.

The punctuated equilibrium model suggests that the time it takes for a firm to respond will vary depending on what period in the firm's change cycle is being examined. For the majority of a firm's history, the management will be slow to change its structures and practices in response to environmental change, regardless of how well it has been performing or its prior performance (Tushman and Romanelli 1985). During revolutionary periods, however, significant changes in strategies and structures will occur during a relatively short period of time. During these transformation periods, individuals in the firm will feel a high degree of discomfort and a need to come to an agreement on some new order. Significant change may occur quickly.

In the management literature, no theoretical or empirical work has yet been completed that addressed how much time a firm takes to respond to the need for change. The purpose of the research in this book was to address this issue.

Below is a detailed description of the punctuated equilibrium model. It is divided into three sections, strategic orientation, convergent periods, and forces for change.

Strategic Orientation

When a firm is founded it establishes a strategic orientation, which consists of the firm's values, strategies, power distribution, control systems, and organizational structure. A body of research argues that there must be consistency between all aspects of a firm's strategic orientation and the industry requirements in order for the firm to achieve superior financial performance. These researchers (for example, Lawrence and Lorsch 1967) contend that the degree of consistency between these aspects of the firm's orientation, strategy and environment determines the firm's financial performance.

This literature contends that the firm's management first chooses a strategy that fits the demands of the environment. The choices of structure and of the distribution of power and control are determined by the choice of strategy. High-performing organizations, researchers argue, are those that have developed specialized units to deal with those tasks that are critical to the success of the firm. For example, firms that have identified customer service as critical have developed a separate department for customer service that reports directly to a senior executive. Further, an organization that is pursuing a strategy of developing the most innovative products will develop a structure that will be more decentralized than firms that are pursuing a low-cost leadership strategy.

In addition, the more complex the interdependence is between different functional departments, the more complex the integrating mechanisms that are required for effective performance. Moreover, the nature of the control system should be based on the critical tasks of the subunits. For tasks that are difficult to evaluate, the firm needs to adopt more flexible control systems, emphasizing social control processes such as a strong organization culture.

When a firm changes its strategy, other elements of the organization's configuration must change if the strategy is to be implemented as intended. Much of this literature contends that because senior executives do not know the optimal configuration, they experiment, thus gradually moving toward the optimal configuration by experimenting with small, incremental changes.

To summarize, this literature argues that a firm's financial performance is a consequence of the extent to which (1) the strategic orientation is consistent with the demands of the environment, and (2) the structure, control systems, and organization processes support, or are consistent with, the strategic orientation.

Convergent Periods

The punctuated equilibrium model contends that for most of a firm's history, it will experience periods of stability, or convergence, during which it maintains its existing strategic orientation. There is no change in the firm's basic organizational activity patterns. During these periods, inertia forces increase and firm members increasingly come to ignore developments in their competitive environment that should signal the need to alter the firm's strategic orientation. Major change is actively prevented (Gould 1989).

If small, incremental changes occur during a convergent period, their purpose is to achieve greater consistency in the firm's internal operating practices. During this period, the organization formalizes the rules and authority relationships throughout the formal structure. In addition, a set of social and political activities are developed that support the firm's strategic orientation and provide external and internal legitimization to its stakeholders. Externally, the organization builds webs of relationships with buyers, suppliers, and financial backers. Management makes commitments to external constituents in return for its support of their objectives. These relationships tend to hinder the firm's ability to assess environmental opportunities and threats. Even if someone recognizes the need for change, it becomes more difficult for management to disrupt the external relationships with these resource providers.

The firm's culture is included in this set of social activities. Culture involves the firm's core values and beliefs as to how the firm operates. This is an important method of control used by organizations. Newly hired employees go through formal and informal orientation and training programs in which they are taught how they are to behave and what frameworks to use to make decisions. These people are rewarded and promoted at least partially on the basis of how well they embody the firm's culture. Over time, the organization's culture and behavior patterns become institutionalized. These social and structural processes facilitate the execution of the existing strategic orientation. Further, because firm members accept the values and behavior as rules that are seldom questioned, the firm is less able to identify changes that have occurred in the environment.

During these relatively long periods of time, incremental change only moves the structures, control systems, and strategies toward ever-increasing coalignment with the firm's strategic orientation (Tushman and Romanelli 1985). The key players in the organization during this time period are the mid-level managers. Performance is the consequence of both choosing the appropriate activities and achieving consistencies among the organization's activities. Inconsistent behaviors and activities can be expected to lead to poorer performance.

Forces for Change

Tushman and Romanelli (1985) identified internal and external forces that push an organization to change its strategy. The external forces include the evolution of product life cycle, government deregulation, new technology, and the emergence of new competitors. The most basic force is change in the industry demand for a product. The level of industry demand determines the availability and importance of economies of scale and scope. Technology is also a major determinant of the evolution of an industry. Technology evolves through its own life cycle, progressing through stages of emergence, consolidation, maturity, decline, and replacement (Sahal 1981).

Executive leadership must mediate between the internal and external inertia forces and the environmental forces requiring change. It is the firm's executive's responsibility to decide to take action and implement strategic reorientation. However, the incumbent management often fails to initiate a reorientation, even if the need for change is apparent. There are many case examples that document how major change only occurs after the company founder dies or existing executives are replaced by managers from outside the organization. These outside managers have few ties to the existing order. In some cases it is other participants in the corporate governance process who will force the firm's executives to initiate a reorientation; these include large shareholders, corporate raiders, and the firm's board members.

We found that the punctuated equilibrium model provided an excellent framework to describe the behavior of the firms that we observed during the period of 1983 through 1996. The reorientation concept captures the magnitude of changes that must be made to change an organization's strategic direction. For the firm to maintain a fit between its strategy, structure, and systems, major changes in strategy are likely to be accompanied by changes in other elements of the organization's design.

2

The Role of Financial Performance

Massive change is not an activity that firms approach lightly or very often. History is littered with examples of firms that continued doing business as they always had despite a steady erosion in their financial performance. Almost without fail, companies will wait until they experience a crisis that forces them to overcome inertia and initiate a reorientation. Many of the 100 firms we investigated did initiate massive change, but they did so with very different response times. We set out to discover which relationships influence the time it takes a firm to initiate a reorientation.

The first relationship was fairly straightforward. If a firm experienced several years of poor performance (as measured by a comprehensive measure of performance) or a sharp decline in its overall financial health, it initiated a reorientation quickly. The few exceptions to this trend are important because they increase our understanding of what factors might help firms to become proactive. Our case study of General Mills, which is discussed later in this chapter, is a prime example. Far more often than not, large companies experienced five, six, or even ten years of poor performance before they finally implemented a new strategic direction.

The second relationship to affect the reorientation time frame involved the key participants in the governance structure. Once again we found several patterns that emerged from our investigation, which are discussed in greater detail in Chapters 4 and 5.

PERFORMANCE AS A CONDITION OF
REORIENTATION

Why does a firm have to get to the point of bankruptcy or face the threat of a hostile takeover before instituting major changes? Too often, such a crisis is required to overcome objections from the people who are resistant to change. Many researchers have found that firm failure is extremely important, as Geswick observed, in "setting the stage for revolution" (1991, 22).

Stuart Slatter (1984) examined a sample of firms that had experienced a financial turnaround. He found that in a crisis, people act quickly. However, the window of opportunity was limited. If the firm waited until a severe financial crisis occurred, few actions could save it. Three in four turnarounds failed because the firms waited to act until the financial situation had become so critical that there were not enough financial resources to avert collapse.

One of the interesting paradoxes of organizational life is that financial success often sets the conditions that lead to eventual failure. Tushman and Romanelli (1985) observed that the longer a firm had experienced successful performance, the stronger were its inertia forces. Executives and employees tended to become complacent and arrogant and to institutionalize the strategies and organizational practices that had led to past successes. If changes occurred in the environment, management was unlikely to notice and instead continued with the current strategy, which they believed had yielded successful outcomes. Successful firms like General Motors, IBM, and Sears were unable to respond in a timely fashion to the changes that were occurring within their respective environments, and each lost billions of dollars in firm market value.

This phenomenon of inertia has been called "the success syndrome" (Nadler, Shaw, and Walton 1995, 10). If the firm is able to maintain a long period of financial success, it increasingly will become internally focused and organization members will increasingly rely on the existing set of practices that led to the past successes. For example, International Business Machines (IBM) continued to rely on its mainframe computers after it became increasingly clear that the market was instead moving to personal computers, software, and networking. A firm can become defensive, blaming problems on external factors not under management's control. This denial leads it to rely even more heavily on past practices. If this cycle continues and financial performance continues to decline, the firm can move into a downward spiral that can lead to eventual failure.

Successful firms enjoy the "luxury" of denial and are able to react slowly to problems because they have been able to build excess financial resources, or financial slack (Cyert and March 1963). This provides a buffer that allows firms to "wait and see" if changes in the environment are significant and permanent. Slack reduces the manager's urgency to

change because it allows the firm to maintain its current level of performance even in the face of changes in its competitive environment (Meyer
1982). Managers of such firms view environmental changes as less threat-
ening, and so will normally be slower to initiate a reorientation.

Learning Theory

Learning theory explains how prior financial performance in organizations affects management's decision to initiate major change. Cyert
and March (1963) were the first to argue that managers use prior performance as a standard against which to measure their aspirations.
Managers develop their aspirations by examining the performance of
comparable organizations and determining the desires of the firm's
dominant coalition or owners.

If there is a gap between the managers' targeted goals and actual outcomes, managers will interpret this result as a signal of either success or
failure. If negative outcomes persist, it will lead to a greater likelihood of
major change. Cyert and March (1963) argue that if performance does
not meet managers' aspiration levels, they will consider making incremental changes such as cost cutting and establishing tighter control. If
performance improves at this stage, then managers will simply continue
to make minor changes to the firm's standard operating procedures.

Cyert and March (1963) focus on short-term, operational decision
making. However, they did not specifically address decision making in
those situations in which the organization's standard operating practices are no longer useful. In an extension of the Cyert and March (1963)
model, Grinyer and McKiernan (1990) argued that if minor adjustments
in standard operating procedures fail to improve performance, then a
fundamental change in a firm's strategies, structures, and systems will
be considered. Our research offers an extension to this model by adding
the dimension of time. We found that the longer a firm experienced poor
performance and the more severe the change in prior financial performance relative to the firm's competitors, the faster the firm initiated reorientation. These results confirm the importance of the learning model
framework and extend the framework by adding the dimension of time.
It appears that prior performance is used by managers as a signal to indicate whether the organization's practices need to be altered. Managers
learn from their experience, so continuing failure should increase the
likelihood of changes in a firm's strategies, structure, and systems.

We found evidence to indicate that managers use different measures
of performance when considering different time frames and types of actions. When a simple measure, such as average return on assets or a decline in return on assets, was used, it had no impact on reducing the time
it took for managers to initiate a reorientation. In such cases, the slack

resources of large, established corporations may allow executives of these firms to attribute the declines in return on assets as a temporary situation, which poses no threat. We found in our sample that management too often did not take action; consequently, the situation only got worse. Management should take any decline in performance as a signal to consider the possibility that the firm's strategic orientation may no longer be appropriate. The current business environment is too competitive for firms to respond slowly to clear signals such as declines in performance.

However, we found that if managers used a comprehensive measure of prior performance, it established a much greater sense of urgency to make comprehensive change. Altman's Z is one such comprehensive measure. It consists of five financial ratios: working capital divided by total assets, retained earnings divided by total assets, earnings before interest and taxes divided by total assets, market value of common and preferred stock equity divided by total liabilities, and sales divided by total assets (Altman 1971). This measure is an accurate predictor of bankruptcy for manufacturing firms and can be used as a measure of a firm's overall financial well-being (Chakravarthy 1986). If this composite measure declines from year to year, the firm's managers should view it as an important indicator that the firm needs to change the alignment of its practices to its environment.

Two of the ratios included in the calculation of Altman's Z—working capital divided by total assets and equity divided by total liabilities—indicate how much slack a firm has. If the firm's Altman's Z value has been declining for several years, this will indicate to the firm's executives that slack resources are declining and reorientation should be initiated more quickly.

A second important result that we found was that the steepness in the decline of the Altman's Z measure affected the speed with which a reorientation was implemented. Surprisingly, few past studies have investigated the influence of the severity of the decline in prior performance on the magnitude of change implemented by managers. Grinyer, Mayes, and McKiernan (1988) examined the point at which firms experiencing a steep performance decline will respond by implementing massive change. In our study, we found that increases in the sharpness of the decline in performance reduce the time until which the executives defined the situation as being a crisis and implemented a reorientation.

In summary, for the majority of cases that we examined, if the firm experienced several years of poor performance (measured by Altman's Z), this led to a quicker reorientation. Several of these cases are discussed in later chapters. However, firms that had been enjoying superior financial performance relative to the industry initiated reorientations more slowly. We did find several interesting exceptions to this latter finding, which are reviewed because they provide a model of how firms can most successfully respond to changes in their environment. One of the cases (reviewed in Chapter 4), Cummins Engine, initiated a reorientation even before the firm's financial performance had started to decline. This was due to the vision and drive of a charismatic chief executive officer. The second example is General Mills, which initiated a reorientation while continuing to be managed by a long-tenured chief executive officer. This case is important because the reorientation was accomplished with minimal disruption in the corporate governance process. Most important, the firm was able to achieve superior financial results immediately following the reorientation.

General Mills: A Model to Follow

General Mills provides us with an interesting example in which long-tenured internal managers came to recognize the need for a comprehensive organizational change. They developed and implemented a plan before pressures from poor performance or external participants in the governance process, such as stockholders, intervened to trigger a reorientation.

Incumbent management implemented the reorientation within a short time frame in comparison to the other firms in our sample. The managers became convinced that the existing strategy was not consistent with investors' performance objectives even though the firm was still obtaining above-average financial returns for shareholders (compared to the Standard & Poor averages). However, the firms lead in performance in relation to its competitors in the food industry was rapidly declining.

History

General Mills had little experience at restructuring. After World War II, the company decided to leave its historical roots (the low-margin flour industry) and begin to develop higher-margin, branded food products. The firm continued with this chosen strategic orientation for forty years.

At the end of 1968 the retiring chief executive officer chose James McFarland to become his successor. McFarland perceived that the food industry was becoming mature. At this time, the stock market was evaluating food companies as low-growth companies and assigning them a low price-earnings ratio. Investors preferred capital gains from their investments rather than dividends. The General Mills corporate management was only too eager to meet the shareholders' desire for sales growth.

McFarland set aggressive growth targets, which he intended to meet by embarking on a program of diversification. Also, as was typical of most executives, he wanted to maintain his independence from the capital markets. He did not want to finance new acquisitions with debt or issuing new stock. McFarland was able to utilize the cash flows from the food product markets to finance the acquisitions with some added use of debt financing. McFarland also was committed to creating stable earnings for General Mills by transforming it into the "all-weather growth company" (Donaldson 1994, 94).

McFarland created venture teams to find new opportunities, which eventually led to quite a few acquisitions. A system was put in place that gave incentive to managers who created the most deals. Sales increased at a compound rate of 14 percent annually and earnings per share grew at 13.5 percent, outperforming the general market as well as competitors in the food industry.

Under McFarland's reign General Mills acquired toys, games, apparel, specialty retailing, travel services, and stamp and rare coin businesses. When McFarland retired in 1976, the new chief executive officer, E. R. Kinney, began a period of consolidation and improved efficiency. He established tighter corporate control systems and charged each division for its use of corporate capital. Like McFarland did with him, Kinney personally selected his successor. In 1981, the new chief executive officer was Bruce Atwater, a twenty-three-year veteran of the consumer products division who had worked closely with Kinney.

Atwater's Reorientation

Atwater and Kinney, with active encouragement from the board, chose Mark Willes, former president of the Federal Reserve Bank of Minneapolis, as the new chief financial officer. They wanted to emphasize the importance of the financial aspects of management. The board and management of General Mills were worried by Wall Street's increasing concern with General Mills's unfocused diversification. The toy and fashion businesses were subject to sharp cyclical swings in financial performance, and the food product lines were continuously being called on to "bail out" the poor performance of the other corporate divisions. Atwater and Kinney felt that, given the changes that were occurring in the financial markets, there was a need to bring a strong external capital-market perspective to corporate decision making.

Atwater faced a problem, though: he had to convince the managers under him that the need for change was urgent. As a new chief executive officer, especially one who had been selected from inside the organization, he had to be careful not to destroy their trust, which would be hard to restore. Somehow he had to build a perceived need for change throughout the organization.

Even before he took the helm, Atwater may have already developed the strategic direction in which he wanted to take the firm. In his first letter to shareholders, in 1981, he announced that he would double capital expenditures and would spend 75 percent of the budget on the core businesses of food and restaurants. This was a clear signal of his intent to change the strategic course of General Mills.

To begin to build a need for change within the organization, Atwater took two important preliminary steps. First, he created a task force that examined the corporate diversification strategies of the best-performing firms in the United States. The conclusion of the study confirmed management's (and Wall Street's) suspicion that the more diversified the company, the more "average" the performance. The majority of the top performers were concentrated in only one or two industries. At this time General Mills was involved in five industries and was known as being a slow, methodical, bureaucratic decision maker.

With the encouragement of Mark Willes, the new chief financial officer, Atwater introduced a new management incentive system in 1981. The past incentive system was based only on earnings per share. The new system was more balanced, giving managers bonuses based equally on growth in earning per share and return on equity. Splitting the focus equally between growth and return on equity was a clear and unequivocal signal that the chief executive cared as much about superior returns on shareholder investment as he did about corporate continuity and growth. That major shift of emphasis prepared the ground for the changes to come.

A significant change in the external environment occurred in 1984, which gave Atwater the managerial discretion to move the organization more quickly toward a new strategic orientation. In 1984, as a result of changes occurring in the toy and fashion industry environments, General Mills experienced its first serious downturn in financial performance.

The corporate executives of General Mills had great difficulty understanding the fashion and toy businesses since their background was in the less dynamic food business. General Mills's toy business consisted of Parker, Kenner Products, and Fundimensions, which generated less than $800 million in annual sales. Parker had been purchased for its product line of well-known board games, which was being hurt by the electronic and video game market (which Parker had been late in entering). Once it did enter, however, it experienced a sales boom, producing $225 million of game cartridges in fiscal 1983. Then the home video market fell apart, hardware makers closed up shop, and game companies flooded the market, driving prices down. In just one year (1984), instead of selling $225 million, Parker sold only $117 million, and the situation only got worse. The operating return on assets for toys fell from 23 percent to 13 percent, and in 1985, sales of video games virtually disappeared (Beam and Dobrzynski 1985).

General Mills's fashion clothing business fared no better. The fashion industry was also becoming more competitive and required faster changes to meet the demanding tastes of the public. Its Izod clothing division rode the crest of a "preppy" wave to a record $400 million only to see sales decline to about $225 million in 1985. This occurred from a glut of lower-priced look-alikes on the U.S. market as well as a shift in consumer preference away from solid-knit shirts (Mehler 1985).

This was the "crisis" that Atwater needed to kick his change agenda into high gear. It established the need for major change clearly in the minds of all stakeholders and set the stage for the reorientation that occurred in 1984 and 1985. In 1984, Atwater altered the corporation's primary structure. The many different businesses were consolidated into five major core product groups—consumer foods, restaurants, toys, fashion, and specialty retailing. This prepared the ground for the 1985 announcement that General Mills would refocus on only the food and specialty restaurant businesses. Additionally, General Mills split its consumer food group, which accounted for 67 percent of total sales, into two segments: grocery products and convenience/international foods. The new structure would allow management to better focus attention on General Mills's brands.

The *1985 Letter to Shareholders* announced that the firm would be moving to a much more focused diversification strategy. It confirmed that the core business of General Mills was the production and distribution of packaged convenience foods, which "was[,] and still is, a highly profitable and stable business." The commitment to this more focused strategy became clear in the 1985 annual report. The firm announced that two separate companies would be set up—Kenner Toys and Crystal Brand—sand that the stock for these two businesses would be distributed to General Mills shareholders.

Atwater stated that his goal was to reach a 6 percent real annual growth rate. To do this he was relying on two mature, slow-growth industries. Packaged foods were only growing at 1 percent a year, and the restaurant industry was growing at 3 percent. Atwater stated his intention to develop a new corporate culture, one that encouraged managers to take more initiative and become "more entrepreneurial" (*1985 Letter to Shareholders*).

The results of the corporate restructuring began to be felt in 1986 with General Mills experiencing double-digit sales and profit increases in its consumer foods and restaurant divisions. In mid-1986, the company completed its streamlining when it sold its furniture group, which included the Pennsylvania House and Kittenger furniture operations. Fashion and specialty retailing revenues rose only 3.4 percent, but continuing operations shot up 28 percent after General Mills sold four of the six businesses in the group. In the 1986 annual report, General Mills announced plans to invest money gained from divestitures into strengthening new consumer food products and expanding its restaurant holdings, which were led by Red Lobster Inns of America and two smaller, ethnic-based chains—Olive Garden (Italian) and Leeann Chin (Chinese).

Corporate management made the decision to invest two more years into the specialty retailing business in an attempt to build its scale and management capability. After two years, if it had not reached its growth and profitability objectives, the business would be spun off. The planned refocusing was completed in May 1988 with the sale of the remaining specialty retailing businesses—Talbots, to JUSCO (Japan), and Eddie Bauer, to Spiegel, for combined gross proceeds of $585 million.

Aftermath: Success

When, on January 28, 1985, Atwater announced the decision to divest the toy and fashion groups, the two-day market-adjusted return was an astounding 12.8 percent increase. The response on January 7, 1988, when the sale of Talbots and Eddie Bauer was announced, was another 4 percent increase. The result of the successful implementation of this reorientation was that the return on shareholder equity increased from 16.7 percent in 1980 to 56.6 percent in 1989. There could be little doubt that General Mills had chosen the correct strategic orientation.

Since General Mills had been slower than its rivals to move overseas, Atwater decided to establish joint ventures with well-established international food companies in an attempt to catch up. Consequently, in 1989, it set up a promising new venture with Nestlé, S.A., called Cereal Partners Worldwide.

The outstanding level of financial performance continued. Through 1993, Atwater could boast that he had earned the highest return on equity of any firm in its industry. General Mills averaged 43 percent for the period of 1989 through 1993, versus an industry average of 17 percent. In 1992, General Mills continued its strategy of finding international partners by joining Pepsico and Nestlé in creating the largest snack food company in Europe (called Snack Ventures Europe). Sales in fiscal 1993 reached $750 million and were forecast to hit $2 billion by the year 2000.

In 1994, Atwater, nearing retirement, announced to General Mills's shareholders the name of his successor and his plans to spin off the restaurant business. The new company would be called Darden Restaurants, with 1994 sales of $3.2 billion. It had become clear that both businesses, restaurant and cereal, were being faced with increases in competition and a further slowdown of market demand. Additionally, analysts had long complained that the restaurant business ate up too much corporate cash for capital expenditures. The restaurant business was generating about 25 percent of corporate earnings, but it was using 50 percent of corporate capital expenditures. Now this money could be used to overhaul the $5.5 billion food business manufacturing and distribution system.

The *1996 Letter to Shareholders* announced that General Mills had experienced an 8 percent increase in sales, a 21 percent return on shareholders' equity and almost $200 million in free cash flow. General Mills had become a very focused, cash-rich market leader in the food industry.

Conclusion

This is a unique case in which the incumbent management was able to see the need for change before the financial performance deteriorated below industry averages. Out of our sample of firms, General Mills was one of the fastest firms to initiate a reorientation. In addition, General Mills was able to achieve very successful financial results immediately following the reorientation.

In the majority of the cases we examined, financially underperforming firms were forced to implement radical change. These firms normally experienced poor financial performance for at least five years before a reorientation was implemented. In addition, many of these firms took three to five years after the reorientation was implemented before they were able to achieve acceptable levels of financial performance.

This case provides an important "ideal" model as to how incumbent management should respond. Atwater was very successful at overcoming internal resistance to change before any perceived prolonged crisis had occurred. His first important step, with the help of Wilkes, was the implementation of a management incentive system that focused on shareholder value. This changed the way managers made their capital-budgeting decisions. Moreover, Atwater's directive that a study be conducted to determine the characteristics of the best-performing firms helped to fuel the organization's growing dissatisfaction with the firm's current diversification strategy.

3

The Role of the Chief Executive Officer and Top Management Team Members

There have been many stories in the popular press describing the power of executives to control the lives of thousands of employees and billions of dollars in assets. Executives, especially the chief executive officer (CEO), have a critical role in determining the behavior and outcomes of organizations (Chandler 1962; Hambrick and Mason 1984).

Researchers see a firm's executives as the key mediators between inertia and forces for change (Mintzberg 1978). The executive team must intervene when internal and external forces pressure a firm to maintain the status quo, often in spite of clear adverse consequences. The forces that cause firms to change stem from competitors, changes in consumer tastes, government regulations, and changes in the expectations of the firm's internal and external stakeholders.

Chandler (1962) found evidence that market opportunities determined firm strategy and, in turn, determined the firm's structure and operating practices. Others have identified product life cycles, technology, and changes in the social, political, and legal environments as examples of environmental modifications that cause significant changes within organizations (Grinyer, Mayes, and McKiernan 1988; Meyer 1982; Tushman and Romanelli 1985). However, these environmental changes create a need for organizational change but do not in themselves trigger a revolution (Geswick 1991). It is clear that the magnitude of change required for a reorientation requires decisive action by the executives, board members, or shareholders if the firm is to be able to overcome its inertia forces. We found that in most cases it is the chief executive officer who initiated and directed the strategic reorientations.

It makes sense that the chief executive officer would be pivotal in bringing about change. He or she is the individual most likely to possess the power and managerial discretion necessary to translate a need for change into organizational outcomes. No one else has the same legal authority and responsibility in the corporation. The chief executive officer is responsible for developing strategy and organizational practices so that the organization meets its objectives (Brady and Helmich 1984).

In this chapter we review three different roles that executives have had in relation to the time taken for the firms we observed to initiate a reorientation. First, long-tenured chief executive officers, by and large, did not implement a reorientation even though they continued to experience poor performance. If the firm did initiate a reorientation, it was only after a new executive from another firm was named to the position. All evidence indicates that the board of directors and shareholders of these firms were unable to pressure the existing management into implementing fundamental change. The only choice for the board was to find an executive from outside the firm who was not committed to the firm's existing strategies.

We review two case examples, AlliedSignal and Tenneco, which describe how massive change resulted after the hiring of outside chief executive officers. In the case of AlliedSignal, the first reorientation was implemented relatively quickly, but for seven years it proved unsuccessful, a trend that was only reversed when an outside chief executive was brought into the firm.

The second example is Tenneco. For ten years, Tenneco did not go through a reorientation even though it continued to experience poor performance. When the board finally did act, it appointed a new chief executive officer from outside the firm, who immediately implemented a reorientation.

Second, we found that the fastest companies to initiate a reorientation were those in which the existing chief executive officer was able to see the need to respond while the firm was still experiencing superior financial results. However, the phenomenon can be considered rare since we identified only three cases in our sample of 100 firms. The most notable of the three was General Mills (reviewed in Chapter 3). The two others are Baxter Laboratories and Cummins Engine. In the case of Baxter, the chief executive officer had been with the firm for fourteen years but was still able to change (relatively quickly) the firm's strategic orientation in an effort to adapt to major changes in the environment. At Cummins Engine, a charismatic, transformational leader identified an emerging and serious competitive threat from Japanese competitors before they had actually made inroads into the North American market. The CEO was able to initiate a reorientation before the firm's performance had declined and before a major change in the environment had taken place.

Third, and contrary to what we expected, in the majority of the firms we examined, the top management team members were not actively involved in initiating a reorientation. Because of the large size of these organizations, we had expected that the chief executive officer would have to rely on key executives to carry out massive change. Instead, however, we were unable to identify situations where the top management team members (excluding the chief executive officer) influenced the time taken to initiate a reorientation.

OUTSIDE CHIEF EXECUTIVES

In the majority of large U.S. corporations, the incumbent chief executive officer selects his or her successor. Several years before reaching the firm's mandatory retirement age, the incumbent chief executive chooses an executive from the current management team who is identified as the likely successor. This executive is often given the position of president and chief operating officer. Assuming that this executive performs well in the president's position for the next two to three years, when the incumbent chief executive officer retires, the title of chief executive officer will be passed to the president. This common succession pattern has been labeled as "healthy," since the baton of corporate leadership is passed smoothly to the new successor with minimal disruption to the organization routine (Vancil 1987).

When the board of directors selects a chief executive from outside the firm, the stock market interprets this behavior as an indication that the firm is having problems. At the very least, the selection of an outside chief executive officer is a signal to the firm's stakeholders that the board of directors desires change (Dalton and Kesner 1983; Friedman and Singh 1989). It makes sense that a chief executive officer from outside will not be constrained by past firm practices, values, and political alliances (Milliken and Lant 1991; Pfeffer 1981). That makes it easier for the new chief executive officer to instigate the kinds of major changes required to initiate a performance turnaround (Starbuck and Hedberg 1977; Tushman and Romanelli 1985). In a Columbia University research project, externally recruited executives were found to be three times as likely to initiate frame-breaking change as existing executives (Tushman, Newman, and Romanelli 1986). Frame-breaking change intentionally destroys the firm's existing identity, values, and mission and builds a new frame within which organizational decisions are made.

We found exactly the same pattern. If a new chief executive officer was an insider who has been with the firm for three years or longer, he or she either did not make the necessary changes or made them too slowly to have a positive effect on the firm's performance (during the period of our study). In the Tenneco case, a major reorientation happened only when the board finally took action and brought in an outside successor. This new chief executive officer wasted little time initiating a reorientation, and as a result, the corporation shed many of its unrelated businesses and was able to obtain consistent returns on equity of 20 percent or more.

Another example of successful reorientation under a new, outside chief executive is Polaroid, which is discussed in Chapter 5. In this instance Polaroid's incumbent chief executive had initiated a reorientation only to prevent a takeover attempt by Shamrock Holdings. The firm changed its corporate strategy from an instant camera company and redefined itself as being in the electronic imaging business. This proved to be a disastrous strategy that subsequently was reversed only when the first outside chief executive officer in Polaroid's history was brought in.

The third example, AlliedSignal, is outlined here because, like Polaroid, the firm initiated a reorientation soon after it began to experience poor performance. It began to diversify from its primary market, chemicals, into aerospace, electronics, and automotive parts. In 1984-1985, Allied purchased Bendix and merged with Signal. The new company consistently underperformed the industry average financially. By 1991, Allied was in serious financial trouble and experiencing a substantial negative cash flow. Only when the firm faced this major financial crisis did the board name a new chief executive officer. This executive, who was hired from General Electric, immediately initiated a second reorientation that strategically refocused the firm.

AlliedSignal: It Took an Outside Successor

In 1979, Edward L. Hennessy Jr. succeeded Joseph Collinson as chief executive officer of Allied. Hennessy, had spent three years in a seminary intending to become a priest, but he realized it was not his calling and started a new career as a junior accountant at Price Waterhouse. In 1950, Hennessy began climbing the management ladder. He joined Textron and at the same time enrolled in Fairleigh Dickinson University. There he studied business, graduating in 1955. He joined ITT, where he became one of Harold Geneen's "whiz kids" and a disciple of Geneen's asset management theories. He then moved to Colgate-Palmolive as director of finance for Europe, the Middle East, and Africa. A year later he joined Heublein and stayed seven years. He then served another seven years at United Technologies, becoming an executive vice president.

When Hennessy became president of Allied in 1979, the company had been performing poorly, largely because of a dependence on its traditional chemical business. Soon after joining the company, Hennessy started to identify the areas in which Allied could expand. Over the next five years, he sold off about forty businesses and purchased about $3.8 billion of acquisitions.

In 1984 Hennessy purchased Bendix Corporation. This move delivered the coup de grace to a three-way takeover battle that involved his former boss at United Technologies and Martin Marietta. In 1984, Bendix contributed 39 percent of Allied's $10.7 billion in sales and 64 percent of its $488 million of profits. Hennessey was given credit for his fast and successful integration of Bendix with Allied (Leinster 1985).

Hennessy next acquired the Signal Company. This major move started when Hennessy proposed in 1985 to Signal executives that they consider a joint bid for Hughes Aircraft. The two companies soon realized it would be too difficult to break up a company the size of Hughes. Instead, they began talking about the possible merger of Signal and Allied, which was a better partnership considering that the companies' product lines had much in common. At the time, this merger was the biggest nonoil merger ever accomplished. The new company would be cash rich as well as one of the world's largest high-tech aerospace engineering concerns.

The acquisition of Signal provided Allied with the size it needed to become an aerospace, electronics, automotive, and chemical giant. The new company was expected to have a growth rate of more than 10 percent, compared with Allied's current 8.7 percent. The new AlliedSignal was to provide enough size to be competitive with the rapidly changing technology field. In five years Hennessy had turned Allied from a lackluster $4.3 billion company into a $10.7 billion conglomerate. However, he was to find out that size alone did not equal success.

Reorientation

To make the new integration of Allied and Signal successful, in 1985 Hennessey initiated a reorientation. Since AlliedSignal was now a diverse conglomerate, Hennessey established a corporate strategy that would concentrate on three high-growth areas—aerospace/electronics, automotive, and engineered materials. To implement this strategy, he sold half of the Union Texas Petroleum division to an investment group for $1.4 billion and announced plans to divest an additional $1 billion in assets. More important, AlliedSignal formed the Henley Group, which consisted of thirty-five diverse businesses outside of the three target areas. This group, which had sales of approximately $4 billion, was earmarked to be spun off to shareholders. AlliedSignal chose this simultaneous approach to divesting assets to spare the company the costs in management time, operational disruptions, and personnel unrest that could result from a lengthy, piecemeal divestiture program.

Within the three remaining principal areas of concentration, the electronics and aerospace operations were restructured around product markets and lines. Hennessey eliminated 3,000 overhead positions and launched a corporate-wide effort to improve productivity. This restructuring cost Allied about $725 million, the bulk of which was related to costs associated with the streamlining and restructuring programs and the establishment of the Henley Group. As a result, AlliedSignal had a net loss of $279 million for 1985.

The year before the Signal merger, Allied's net income was $488 million, or $5.03 per share. When Allied announced the Signal merger, CEO Hennessy predicted that earnings per share from the combination would grow from $4 in 1985 to $5 by 1987. Instead, in 1986 the company only earned $3.28 per share in 1986. Profits declined in 1987 by 15 percent, to $515 million, and they continued to decline another 10 percent, to $463 million, in 1988. Allied shareholders must have wondered when, or if, all this asset shuffling would pay off for them. With regard to AlliedSignal's price-earnings ratio, the company trailed the Standard & Poors 500 index by more at this period than it did when Hennessy joined the company. In 1989 profits improved slightly, to $528 million, but by 1990, profits were down to $462 million, and the company had a loss of $273 million in 1991. Allied did poorest in all of the areas Hennessy had identified as key growth areas. As a result, Wall Street criticism reached a crisis point in 1990–1991 a period when Allied was viewed as an unfocused, hodgepodge corporation.

Interestingly, over at the Henley Group (consisting of companies that, Hennessy had determined, had no earnings potential), chief executive officer Michael Dingman had stopped the losses. Until the market crash of 1987, the price of Henley shares stood almost 40 percent higher than when they were issued in 1986. By contrast, Allied's stock had not improved, instead staying at about $45 for eighteen months.

Securities analysts had two complaints concerning Allied's Hennessey. One was that he wasted too much money on corporate airplanes and a fat bureaucracy, and the other was that he spent too much on research and development, which he boosted 70 percent in three years. In addition, AlliedSignal still lacked a strategic focus (Dobrzynski 1987).

Edward Hennessy changed his strategy too many times. He had spent more than $8 billion on acquisitions and had sold operations with sales of more than $7 billion. He moved into health care, information systems, and electronics businesses, and then backed right out of them. In fact, by mid-1987, Hennessy had sold or closed virtually everything he had bought before the 1983 merger with Bendix. In retrospect, it's not surprising that the financial performance of the conglomerate continued to be poor.

Salvation: An Outside Successor

By 1991, debt was equal to 42 percent of capital, while the cash was pouring out. It was clear to all that it was time to change the leadership.

Edward Hennessey was forced to retire eighteen months before the mandatory retirement age, and the board identified an outsider, Lawrence Bossidy, as the new chief executive officer. Bossidy had been vicechairman at General Electric, where he had worked for thirty-four years. He was a devotee of GE Chairman Jack F. Welch Jr.'s "up-or-out" philosophy of conglomerate management, which states that if a division does not meet the corporate performance objectives, it is sold.

On his first day as the new chief executive officer, he was greeted with a company forecast that predicted a negative cash flow of $435 million in 1991 and $336 million in 1992. Within ten weeks, Bossidy launched his restructuring plan. It reduced capital spending by $225 million, reduced the annual dividend to $1.00 a share (from $1.80), put eight small divisions up for sale, cut 6,200 salaried jobs, and combined ten dataprocessing centers into two. As a result, negative cash flow diminished to $190 million in 1991 and rose to a positive $255 million in 1992. Six months after Bossidy's arrival (in June 1991), Allied's stock had jumped 33 percent, to around $40 a share (Stewart 1992).

Analysts at the time questioned whether Bossidy could fix, rather than just sell off, Allied's more mature divisions. For example, Bendix was primarily an auto parts maker and would need substantial capital investment before it could become an effective global competitor.

Bossidy understood the importance of corporate culture. He wanted to achieve the same type of total transformation that had been achieved at General Electric, but he wanted it done in five years instead of ten. He started by forming a leadership committee, composed of Allied's top twelve executives, to develop a corporate vision and corporate objectives. The targets they agreed on included (1) annual gains in productivity and increases in the operating profit margins from 4.7 percent in 1991 to 9 percent in 1994, (2) return on equity to be increased from 10.5 percent to 18 percent over the same period, and (3) working capital turnover to be increased from 4.2 times a year to 5.2 times.

To translate this corporate vision into reality, Bossidy initiated a corporate-wide Total Quality Management Program. Before the end of 1993, he wanted all 90,000 employees to have completed a four-day course in using of tools such as process maps to hunt for unnecessary work and benchmarking to study other companies' success stories. In addition, in 1992, he initiated a corporate-wide effort to overhaul operating processes by concentrating on reducing inventory and also new product development cycle times. He formed cross-company teams to break down company boundaries and established new administrative centers for excellence. In his *1991 Letter to Shareholders*, he explained:

What we want is thorough, top-to-bottom change. We believe firmly that success in the 1990s will involve fundamental changes in how we operate our businesses and in the way each of us understands his or her role in the Company. It will require visible, involved leaders, not simply competent managers; a plausible vision, shared by every employee, of what the enterprise aspires to achieve; and clearly expressed values that shape our behavior. We are committed to making our vision and values the fundamental blueprint that AlliedSignal people will use to reinvent the Company. We are using these ideas to define our actions every day, and we are making them our way of life.

In an important way, the key to reinventing AlliedSignal is our willingness to let go of the old baggage and dead weight of past practices. These must be abandoned before we can accept change and innovation as the rule in all we do. Creative people and challenging new ideas cannot thrive in an atmosphere choked with unyielding precedents and mystifying operating procedures.

Once Allied's cash flow problem was solved, Bossidy planned to make acquisitions again. From now on, acquisitions were to be modest in size and closely related to existing businesses. Bossidy's special focus would be on the development of international partnerships and on acquisitions selected to improve the firm's global position.

Aftermath: A Startling Turnaround

The year 1992 saw a major loss of $712 million due to the restructuring charges. However, in 1993 the company earned $656 million net income. Return on shareholder equity reached almost 31 percent, and the free cash flow was a positive $365 million. Lawrence Bossidy's reorientation had caused a very successful turnaround for AlliedSignal.

The next year, financial performance continued on the upswing. AlliedSignal achieved a 16 percent increase in net income and earnings per share and a 28.9 percent return on shareholder equity. The board of directors was so pleased that it increased Bossidy's salary a dramatic 82 percent, to $2 million a year; guaranteed him a minimum cash bonus of $1.8 million; and gave him two huge stock option grants, which would become worth $100 million if AlliedSignal stock rose by 10 percent a year over the next five years. This made Bossidy one of the highest-paid executives in the United States. The board justified its actions because the market value of the stock under Bossidy had risen from $4.5 billion to $10 billion and return on equity had climbed from 11 percent to almost 30 percent. In exchange for this compensation package, Bossidy promised to stay at Allied until he retired, even though he had become one of the most sought-after chief executive officers in the country. In particular, companies including IBM, Merck, Kodak, and Westinghouse had expressed an interest in him.

Return on equity for 1995 was 26.7 percent, and sales increased 42 percent, to $14.3 billion. Bossidy had been able to achieve growth from a group of businesses that analysts had believed were in mature industries and incapable of growth, especially automobile parts and chemicals. By 1997, Allied's stock price had increased in value 500 percent since 1991. To achieve this reorientation, Bossidy had replaced dozens of top executives and had continuously called for greater growth and productivity. Lawrence Bossidy appears to be far from finished. In a January 11, 1997 interview in *Fortune* magazine, he reported that he was launching an entirely new reorientation. He explained that what had been done in 1991 was for the firm's survival, but that his next reorientation would ensure future prosperity in the new world economy. A global customer is a much more demanding customer. For example, there used to be a thirty-day delivery window in the aerospace industry, but now delivery must be overnight. Bossidy has stated his desire for Allied to become one of world's premier companies by leading in low-cost, premium-quality products.

Two Reorientations, One Success

During the first reorientation, in 1984–1985, Hennessy had brought about a remarkable corporate transformation. He had turned a once-stodgy chemical company with revenues of $4 billion into a major, $12 billion conglomerate. Shortly thereafter, however, while the rest of the American corporations were becoming more focused on related businesses, Hennessey began implementing the opposite strategy. After five years of poor financial performance and continuous purchases and sales of corporate assets, his strategy proved to be unsuccessful.

As a clear signal to all stakeholders that things would change, an outside chief executive officer was brought in to head AlliedSignal. CEO Bossidy used tools gained from his experience at General Electric to accomplish his reorientation. He emphasized the "softer" dimensions of the reorientation, especially corporate culture. By delegating authority and setting tough performance targets, he created a corporate culture with an unrelenting focus on customer satisfaction. Lawrence Bossidy is considered one of the most successful chief executive officers in the United States.

AlliedSignal provides an excellent example of a situation in which the board of directors appointed an outside successor who immediately reversed the strategic orientation of the firm. This case exemplifies our statistical results: it took the board of directors a long time to act, but once they took action, it was usually extremely successful.

LONG-TENURED EXECUTIVES

Long-tenured chief executive officers are often unable to consider new strategic directions. When chief executive officers first enter a firm, they tend to be open-minded, although they may have some preliminary ideas of what strategies and organizational practices are appropriate to the situation (Hambrick and Fukutomi 1991). As the length of tenure of the chief executive officer increases, however, they tend to become more committed to a chosen way of viewing the industry and its problems and opportunities. Chief executive officers are no different from the rest of us. As executives invest their time and energy in pursuit of their selected course of action, they find it increasingly difficult to reverse their direction.

The firm's recent financial performance plays a critical role in influencing the psychological processes that influence the interpretations made by the firm's executives. It would seem logical that executives who see that their companies are failing would look for new approaches. However, the opposite is more often true. Poor firm performance increases psychological forces that reinforce the practices that were used in the past (Milliken and Lant 1991). Various investigators have identified three major psychological forces that may be activated when a firm experiences failure. The first force has been labeled as an escalation of commitment to past organization practices (Staw 1981). Managers often find it difficult to admit responsibility for failure, especially when their strategies have been made public (Salancik 1977). Chief executive officers must meet regularly with stock analysts, company employees, and shareholders to discuss the firm's strategies and plans.

Chief executive officers tend to interpret the current firm's poor performance as an indication that their strategy is not being implemented properly. Hence, they call on their managers to redouble their efforts to accomplish the previously selected strategy, rather than accepting the possibility that the strategy is incorrect (Pfeffer 1981). The second force is the threat rigidity effect. When executives perceive that they may lose their jobs, they are likely to resort to methods they have used in the past rather than look for novel solutions (Staw, Sandelands, and Dutton 1981). Finally, managers who have experienced poor performance may misperceive environmental events by engaging in wishful thinking (Milliken and Lant 1991). Executives will tend to believe that the current failure is due to general economic conditions or some unusual market events that will diminish shortly.

In addition to these psychological forces, the institutionalization of power can be a strong inertia force. An executive has the ability to give raises and promotions as well as to bestow favors on important external stakeholders such as board members. This allows CEOs to use their existing position to expand their power base even further (Pfeffer 1981). The more power executives possess, the more they can block or slow organizational change. One or more of these factors can cause long-tenured executives to resist changing their firms' strategies.

External stakeholders, meanwhile, are not subject to the same psychological forces that cause managers to persist in using past practices (Milliken and Lant 1991). Outside board members and large shareholders are likely to become increasingly frustrated and pressure for a change in strategy or in management.

Tenneco is a good example of a troubled firm with a chief executive officer who either could not see or could not react to obvious warning signs. Tenneco had been a diversified holding corporation that did not initiate a reorientation, even though performance was below the industry average for over ten years. From 1980 through 1990, the return on equity averaged less than 8 percent, with three of those years showing losses. James Ketelsen, a long-tenured president, who controlled Tenneco for thirteen years starting in 1978, seemed unable to believe that his strategy of focusing on farm and construction businesses had proven unsuccessful. He only made incremental changes and insisted on staying with his original strategy until the bitter end. The board of directors might never have replaced him had he not been accused of fraudulent accounting practices. Only then did the board take action and name an outside chief executive officer as the successor.

Tenneco: A Chief Executive Officer with Blinders

Tenneco started business in the 1940s as the Tennessee Gas and Transmission company. The company changed its name in 1966 and shortly thereafter purchased the Kern County Land Company. This put Tenneco into farming, tractor manufacturing (J. I. Case), and the automotive industry (Walker Manufacturing). In 1968 the company acquired Newport News Shipbuilding. By the 1970s this firm was a conglomerate involved in natural gas pipeline operations, construction, farm equipment, agriculture and land development, automotive components, shipbuilding, and packaging.

From 1982 to 1988, financial performance was below industry standards. Until 1985, management had taken only incremental steps to improve the financial picture. Ketelsen, Tenneco's chief executive officer, sold assets to pay down heavy debt and implemented cost-control programs. In 1985, the company underwent a wage and hiring freeze.

During 1986 and 1987, probably because Tenneco was rumored to be a takeover candidate, Ketelsen took more aggressive restructuring steps. During these years the firm sold its insurance and agriculture business for $1.36 billion. In addition, in 1987 the corporation set up a new structure, a holding company, that would increase financing flexibility and enable it to evaluate subsidiary operations more clearly. Tenneco was reorganized around seven separate business units, and Ketelsen made continuing efforts to cut costs and excess capacity at the farm equipment and automotive parts operations.

Ketelsen took a major step in 1988 to reduce the attractiveness of Tenneco as a takeover target by selling the oil exploration and production operations for $7.6 billion. This sale shifted the strategic emphasis of the firm toward a focus on the farm equipment industry. Many investors and analysts had long expected Tenneco to initiate a major restructuring or reorientation. However, few had expected that it would mean that the company's most profitable unit would be sold. Most analysts believed Ketelsen unloaded the gas and oil unit because it could be sold the quickest and the proceeds could thus be used to reduce debt and stave off takeover attempts.

The strategy failed, and financial performance in 1989 did not improve. Ketelsen promised shareholders that he would sell slow-growing businesses with the exception of J. I. Case, the farm equipment division. He was determined to invest and expand in the tractor business despite continued dismal returns. From 1983 to 1989, Ketelsen poured more than $2 billion in cash generated from other Tenneco operations into Case's operations. Nonetheless, Case was unable to make inroads against a key rival, Deere and Co. Deere's market share actually increased during this period (from 45 percent to 49 percent), versus Case's unchanged 32 percent share.

Many Wall Street investment managers were getting impatient with Ketelsen and were clamoring for a more massive change in the firm's strategic orientation. By this time Ketelsen had held the reins of Tenneco for nine years yet had little to show in terms of financial performance. During 1989 Tenneco's stock was trading at the $48 a share level, which represented only 62 percent of Tenneco's breakup price.

The following year brought little change as Ketelsen continued to consolidate and eliminate excess capacity. Ketelsen took two steps to improve shareholder value—a $360 million share repurchase program and an increase in the quarterly stock dividend. However, these steps had little effect on building long-term company value.

The situation reached a crisis point in 1991, when Tenneco reported losses of $1 billion, most of it coming from the restructured tractor business. The Case division suffered from a recession in the farm industry as well as internal management problems. In a successful civil litigation, shareholders charged Tenneco's chairman, Ketelsen, and Case's president, James Ashford, with using questionable accounting practices to artificially inflate Case's revenues. Only during this crisis did the board of directors finally take action: it appointed a new management team in September of 1991, naming Michael Walsh as Tenneco's chief executive officer.

Outside Successor, Bold New Direction

Walsh immediately announced a $2 billion restructuring plan. He focused his first actions on reducing the ratio of debt to total capital, which declined from 69 percent at the end of the third quarter to 59 percent at year-end.

In 1992, he began to implement a reorientation that was heavily focused on changing the corporate culture. His steps included centralizing control, establishing tougher performance standards, and installing a company-wide quality management program. He reorganized J. I. Case from a business structure into a functional structure based on engineering, manufacturing, and marketing. He also cut dividends by 50 percent and eliminated 8,000 jobs.

Walsh then announced a new strategic direction. The company would focus on higher returns and less cyclical businesses. He identified packaging, automotive parts, and gas operations as the primary platforms for the future growth. As an indication of this strategy, Walsh initiated two public stock offerings, which raised $750 million and reduced Tenneco's ownership in Case to 44 percent.

In 1995, Tenneco purchased Mobil Oil's plastics division for $1.27 billion and incorporated it into Tenneco's packaging division. This acquisition, which included the Hefty and Baggies product lines, made Tenneco's packaging division the fourth largest in the nation. By the end of 1995, the packaging, automotive, and energy businesses comprised 80 percent of Tenneco's revenues, versus 46 percent in 1992.

By 1996, the strategic restructuring of Tenneco seemed to be complete. The Case division had been completely sold off, and Tenneco announced that it would spin off to shareholders the Newport News Shipbuilding operation, the largest in the world. In addition, Tenneco sold its natural gas operations to El Paso Energy Corporation for $4 billion.

The corporation would now focus on only two businesses—automotive parts (Monroe shocks and Walker exhaust systems) and packaging. Walsh stated that in the future, the company would focus on expanding these businesses globally, accompanied by a new organization structure that was better suited to its emerging worldwide position.

During 1995 and 1996, Tenneco purchased six major specialty manufacturers and two overseas companies to expand its packaging operations, as well as seven major overseas automotive parts manufacturers. In addition, it established large joint ventures—one in China and one with ITT (to develop modular chassis systems for passenger cars and light trucks worldwide). Although this reorientation was late, it appears to have been very successful, with Tenneco reporting returns to stockholders of greater than 20 percent.

As the Tenneco example illustrates, succession is the most important mechanism through which organizations can adapt to environmental changes that have resulted in the firm's poor performance. When a firm is performing poorly, a long-tenured chief executive is likely to be incapable of initiating the needed reorientation. If the board of directors carries out its function properly, it will select a new chief executive officer with the skills and experience necessary to significantly improve the performance of the firm.

PROACTIVE FIRMS

Firms that did not require financial disaster to motivate the initiation of massive change were rare but were the most successful long-term performers. General Electric, Cray Research, and ALCOA all implemented corporate-wide changes ahead of their competition, which allowed them to maintain their superior performance.

Historically, only a small group of high-performing firms has been able to undertake a reorientation without replacing their existing chief executive officer with an outsider. These firms were termed "unusually" proactive, as they initiated their reorientations under conditions of increasing financial success (Virany, Tushman, and Romanelli 1992). These firms seemed able to take advantage of a relatively stable executive team to initiate major change, not to address an organization crisis but rather to enhance their ability to cope with turbulent environmental conditions. Miles and Snow's (1978) prospectors and Miller and Friesen's (1978) adaptive and innovative firms all possess an organization culture and management team that are future oriented and more open to change. Miles and Snow (1978) suggested that their prospect type of firm was continually changing, as well as creating industry change.

At least two conditions must exist for a chief executive officer to be able to successfully initiate change proactively. First, the CEO must be extremely knowledgeable and experienced about the company's product or service. Eisenhardt (1989) found, in her study of strategic decision making in minicomputer firms, that if the executives had "deep personal knowledge" concerning the firm and its environment, management teams could process information faster and make much quicker strategic decisions. Baker and Cullen (1993) found that executives who had dealt with major change successfully in the past would react faster than those who had not been through the process as frequently. This is exactly what we found in our examples of AlliedSignal and Tenneco. In both cases the new chief executive officers, Bossidy and Walsh, had experience in initiating reorientations and were able to react more quickly and more successfully than their predecessors.

The second condition that must exist is that these executives must possess considerable managerial discretion or power in order to overcome the inertia forces. The distribution of power within the firm has an important impact on the rate and direction of strategic change. Observers of corporate behavior have long contended that the possibility of change is largely determined by the amount of support for a change that exists within the power structure at any point in time (Pettigrew 1985).

Before a chief executive can proactively implement massive change, he or she will need to build political support from key members in the corporate governance structure (Pfeffer 1981). As chief executive officers increase their tenure, they are able to hire more loyal executives who are dependent on them for their positions and dissenters can be eliminated (Mintzberg 1983; Pfeffer 1981). In addition, chief executives are able to develop personal relationships with important customers, bankers, and large shareholders (Pfeffer and Salancik, 1978). Last, the chief executive officer is able to influence the selection of new members for the firm's board of directors (Alderfer 1986).

To overcome these forces of resistance, it sometimes requires a dynamic, charismatic leader, or what recent observers call the "transformational leader." Tichy and Ulrich define this type of leader as "one who commits people to action, who converts followers into leaders, and may convert leaders into moral agents" (1984, 240). This type of leader may prove to be necessary for reorientation, especially *before* a crisis occurs (Grinyer, Mayes, and McKiernan 1988; Tushman, Newman, and Romanelli 1986).

We found very few cases in which the incumbent chief executive officer was able to implement proactive reorientation. Two cases are reviewed, Cummins Engine and Baxter Laboratories. In our first case, the incumbent chief executive officer had extraordinary vision; he foresaw a competitive threat before it materialized. He was able to initiate a reorientation that would take many years of effort before it would be successful. Then, once the reorientation had been implemented, his drive and charismatic personality sold his managment team, board members, and major shareholders on the need to maintain the new strategic direction, despite heavy financial losses.

The second case, Baxter Laboratories, has a very different outcome. Like Cummins Engine, the incumbent chief executive officer initiated a reorientation quickly. It had become clear to firms in the health care industry that massive change would be required if they were to survive. These firms faced the emergence of new cost-conscious, powerful buyers such as health maintenance organizations. Moreover, the federal government was dramatically revising regulations that governed the health care field to encourage cost cutting and competition. The firm's reorientation transformed Baxter into a diversified, full-line supplier to hospitals. Unlike Cummins Engine, however, the strategic reorientation was not successful and was later reversed.

Cummins Engine: A Charismatic Leader

Cummins Engine is the world's largest independent manufacturer of diesel engines. In 1984 its charismatic leader, Henry Schacht, put a reorientation into motion. The firm continued restructuring for the next ten years in an effort to stay ahead of its aggressive Japanese competition. Although it took until 1995 for Cummins to reestablish a position of sustainable profits, analysts are calling Schacht's strategy successful. As of 1996, Cummins continues to dominate the North American industry for diesel engines.

In 1984, judging from Cummins Engine's financial performance, this firm appeared to be the last candidate to initiate a reorientation. Cummins Engine held a commanding 60 percent share of the U.S. market for heavy-duty diesel truck engines, and it had turned in an outstanding financial performance for its shareholders, producing 12.6 percent return on equity in 1984.

However, the Japanese were preparing to launch an aggressive campaign to enter the U.S. market. Schacht had clearly identified this threat in his *1983 Letter to Shareholders*. He noted that the Japanese were the world's leading vertically integrated, low-cost manufacturers and would follow a low-price entry strategy. He further stated his belief that the Japanese strategy would be to enter the smaller, less differentiated end of the market and move up as their products become established.

Schacht's worst fears materialized even faster than he had thought. Cummins began to get calls in 1984 from its best, longtime customers, who stated that they were testing medium-duty engines from several Japanese manufacturers, including Komatsu, Mitsubishi, and Nissan Motor. These Japanese engines were to sell for 15 percent to 40 percent below Cummins's prices.

Schacht knew that if the Japanese gained a foothold in medium engines, heavy engines would be next. At the same time, Cummins itself was trying to break into the medium-duty market and had just launched four new engines. Even though Cummins had just turned in its best year in its history, Schacht made the decision to react immediately to the threat of the Japanese competition and dropped its prices on the new medium-duty engines to meet the Japanese prices. Of all the firms that we examined in this study, Schacht moved the fastest to initiate a reorientation. By dramatically reducing prices below the firm's cost to produce them, he created a "crisis" that would force the organization to significantly improve productivity and quality or else lose millions of dollars of stockholder money. Schacht admitted that the stockholders would lose money but nonetheless argued that there would be less loss in the long run than if the firm moved more cautiously and reduced prices only as it found cost savings.

Reorientation

Schacht went to his board of directors and was able to convince it that the firm must match the Japanese prices or else lose 20 to 30 percent of its business. He also convinced the board that the firm would be able to reorganize so that production costs could be lowered to the point where the new, lower prices would again become profitable (Terrien 1988).

In Schacht's *1985 Letter to Shareholders*, he reported a critical decision: no matter what the cost, he would deny the Japanese a foothold in the U.S. market. To ensure this, Cummins would lower its prices up to 40 percent on its three most popular and newest engine families. Schacht argued that if Cummins blocked Japanese manufacturers, they would find it difficult to penetrate U.S. markets, especially because his firm was committed to maintaining technical superiority. Additionally, he stated that efforts to reduce costs and continuously improve quality and delivery would allow Cummins to reach target profit margins on all new products, even at the much lower prices.

Schacht was able to sell his vision, not only to his board members, but also to shareholders, Wall Street analysts, and suppliers. Using extensive statistical analysis to support his strategy, Schacht convinced everyone that Cummins had to make a preemptive strike against an invasion of low-cost imports and slashed Cummins's prices to save its number one position in the $2 billion North American heavy-duty diesel market.

Schacht would stay focused on diesel engines, but he recognized the need to broaden the Cummins product line into areas that were less mature. Beginning in late 1984, he announced a commitment to become a leader in medium-duty engines for delivery trucks, pleasure boats, and power generators. At this time Cummins was only a minor player in this market. Cummins landed a number of important contracts, including a deal with the school bus manufacturer Blue Bird that could ultimately produce sales of 15,000 engines a year. He also expanded overseas sales, especially in Britain and India (a segment that still represented only a very small portion of the company's total sales).

Along with price slashing and product repositioning, Schacht made changes in how the firm's work was organized. He quickly embraced such Japanese techniques as just-in-time inventory management and flexible manufacturing systems. Actually, Cummins Engine had begun to use a team management approach on its production floor in 1974, whereby assembly workers were organized into teams of ten to thirty people. Each team was responsible for scheduling shifts, ordering materials, and even hiring more workers when necessary.

Now, as part of the reorientation, Schacht used these teams in even more important ways. He assigned them responsibility for finding ways to slash production costs. The teams also were used to break down the traditional rigid assembly lines at a number of Cummins's plants. Instead of only building one product, workers would be required to quickly reset the production line to meet the demand for different products.

Over the next few years, production plants were consolidated and 3,400 out of 13,000 jobs were eliminated. In addition, Schacht spent more than $1 billion on plant and equipment. Much of Cummins's U.S. output was shifted from its old, high-wage manufacturing base in southern Indiana to non-union plants in the South and elsewhere, and even in Indiana, a contract with the Diesel Workers, a company union, conceded that new hires would receive only $12 an hour counting fringe benefits, less than half the $30 enjoyed by senior workers.

In mid-1985, ALCOA directors began discussing the possibility of a merger with Cummins Engine. ALCOA's primary purpose was to get Schacht as chairman of the combined companies. However, Cummins and ALCOA failed to reach an agreement, and the deal soon fell apart.

Results: Late but Not Too Late

In 1987–1988, while Schacht was watching out for the Japanese, a new, fierce, innovative domestic competitor emerged. Detroit Diesel, once a relatively unsuccessful former unit of General Motors, was being rejuvenated under the leadership of auto-racing giant Roger S. Penske. The result was that Detroit Diesel introduced a ground-breaking series of electronically controlled diesel engines which was far superior to anything Cummins Engine had to offer. These engines delivered dramatically better fuel efficiency and boasted nifty computerized features for diagnosing mechanical problems and monitoring driver productivity. In 1992, Detroit Diesel experienced a stunning increase in market share of almost 400 percent, to roughly 22 percent. Only in late 1990 was Cummins able to come to market with its own line of electronic, heavy-duty diesel engines.

With regard to the Japanese, Cummins's aggressive pricing strategy seemed to have worked. In 1990 there were almost no Japanese diesel truck engines sold in the United States. However, this strategy ravaged Cummins's short-term profits. For ten years, the company took investors on a roller-coaster ride, with profits reaching a high of $188 million in 1984 and then plunging to a loss through 1990. Cummins lost more than $200 million in 1988 through 1990.

The turnaround took much longer than the Cummins executives had expected. First, as is typical in major restructuring, the managers seemed always to underestimate both the cost and the time involved. Second, it took the company much longer than predicted to cut its production costs to the level necessary to reestablish its margin after the 1984 decision to cut prices.

Schacht had warned everyone that the company would take a short-term financial hit; still, the negative financial numbers caused big credibility problems. Wall Street analysts and some institutional investors began to criticize his strategy. Schacht became an outspoken critic of Wall Street's fixation on short-term results. In 1989, low profits forced Schacht to mandate across-the-board wage and salary decreases (he cut his own salary by 15 percent). Schacht also faced the prospect of large investors purchasing Cummins and eliminating Schacht's strategy before it had a chance to work. Consequently, he had to find investors who were willing to back his vision. To ensure that Cummins would have the financing to continue investing for the future, in 1990 he sold 20 percent of its stock to three customers: Ford, Tenneco, and Kubota. Ford and Tenneco each own 9.3 percent of the stock, Japan's Kubota owns 5 percent, and the founding family (the Millers) owns an additional 4 percent. Schacht reported in the *1990 Letter to Shareholders* that this provided three long-term investors in Cummins, whose presence lent stability to the shareholder base and reassured constituents who had grown apprehensive about Cummins's ability to continue its commitment to the business.

Cummins did not reach a financial turnaround until 1992, when the company earned $67 million. For those stockholders who had the patience to wait, 1993 saw the price of Cummins stock double. In 1994, the company experienced the best year in its history, reaching $253 million profits on $4.7 billion in revenues. This gave stockholders a 26.7 percent return on equity.

After remaining in control of Cummins Engine for twenty-one years, Henry B. Schacht retired in July 1994. Schacht was only fifty- nine years old but decided that it would be best if Cummins could avoid the distractions of a lengthy transition (Kelly 1994). Schacht had the major influence on choosing his internal successor, J. Henderson, who had worked at Cummins for seventeen years.

Henderson's *1995 Letter to Shareholders* announced a continuation of Schacht's strategy. He announced that Cummins had been successful in cutting debt down to 16 percent of capital and stated his plans to launch a very aggressive, $2 billion capital-spending program over the next two years. This program would emphasize the further development of international joint ventures and new product expansion.

Henderson explained that as a result of stringent new emission standards, Cummins would develop new engines and fuel systems as well as investigate opportunities in electronic controls and information technology. He also asserted that a window of opportunity existed in international markets. Indeed, in what some at Cummins must see as sweet revenge, Komatsu (once a competitor) approached Cummins with the request to make mid-range engines for Komatsu's construction vehicle line. Henderson also indicated that Cummins was working with several local equipment suppliers in developing countries including China and India.

Conclusion

Schacht provided Corporate America with an important example. Many old-line U.S. manufacturers facing low-priced international competition have pursued related diversification, shifting their companies into faster-growing fields such as aerospace, electronics, and service businesses, but Schacht stayed with what Cummins knew best: diesel engines. He fought off a Japanese invasion by developing a strategy that required Wall Street to take a long-term view of its investment. He successfully sold his vision of a long-term perspective based on maintaining current market share above profits.

Schacht never lost faith in his strategy, even though many of his shareholders and critics became impatient with the constant flow of losses. When corporate raiders threatened to take over his company, he went out and found long-term investors who agreed with his strategy. It took him ten years of restructuring, including heavy investment in technology and employee training. Production costs were reduced almost 30 percent, and over $2 billion was invested to revamp Cummin's factories and broaden its product line. Moreover, he continued his efforts to expand into new markets, even after initial efforts proved unsuccessful. To this day, Cummins holds the leading market share in North America, and not a single a U.S.-built tractor-trailer is powered by a Japanese-made engine.

Over the ten years from 1985 to 1994, Cummins successfully became much more diversified and global. Heavy-duty truck engines, which accounted for 60 percent of sales in 1985, today account for less than 30 percent. In addition, sales from outside the United States are 43 percent of the firm's total, compared to only 20 percent ten years ago.

However, Schacht's success in fending off the Japanese came at a steep price, as Cummins experienced losses for the entire 1986–1991 period. Schacht's experience shows how difficult it can be for manufacturers to "hang tough." In today's global market, even the best strategy is no guarantee of success. However, Cummins's recent financial results seem to indicate that Schacht's strategy was correct. Over the last two years, Schacht had returned Cummins to what appeared to be sustained profits, suggesting the long-term view may pay off.

The interesting question that remains is whether or not the speed with which the reorientation was initiated was necessary. No one will ever know the answer for certain. Schacht may have been able to move more cautiously, for example, reducing prices only as the firm was able to actually achieve lower production costs. However, he himself would likely argue that he prevented the Japanese from getting a foothold in the U.S. market. Furthermore, he was able to create a crisis condition within his firm, which forced the organization to move quickly to update manufacturing techniques and drastically improve productivity and quality levels.

Baxter Laboratories: A Timely, but Unsuccessful, Reorientation

Baxter is different from the other cases discussed here because it is an example of a firm in which the long-serving chief executive officer initiated a reorientation almost immediately, in the first year its performance declined. He did so as a result of dramatic changes in government policies that encouraged competition and attempted to control medical costs. Unlike at Cummins and General Mills, the change in strategic orientation was unsuccessful.

Baxter, a hospital supply company, was selling products that had lower margins than its competitors, which put it in a very vulnerable competitive position. The chief executive officer, Vernon R. Loucks, responded to this competitive threat in an extremely aggressive and timely manner. He diversified the company's product lines within the health care field and undertook a merger with a firm that was more than two times bigger in sales so that Baxter could become a full-line supplier to its major customer, hospitals. Making the merger and diversification work was much more difficult than company management had thought, and the firm failed to meet its profit expectations over the next eight years. In 1996, the firm split the company into two separate organizations, thus reversing the strategy of the original reorientation.

Competitive Environment

Baxter had developed a very successful strategy during the 1970s, which focused on a few key product lines sold strictly to hospitals. It dominated the markets for these key products through technical innovation, a strategy that worked well as long as hospitals freely accepted Baxter's annual hefty price increases. Up until the end of the 1970s, there were few rewards for suppliers to be cost efficient in the health care industry.

However, beginning in the 1980s, the competitive environment began to change drastically. In 1983, Congress passed Medicare cost-containment rules. Hospitals were now paid fixed amounts for designated treatments under Medicare, regardless of the actual costs a provider incurred. Private insurers soon followed with their own rules to contain medical costs. Moreover private insurance plans and employee benefit programs were restructured to include front-end deductibles and copayments, which placed greater responsibility on individuals to contain their own health care costs. Consumers, as a consequence, began to use their health care benefits much more conservatively. Many consumers began to accept new alternatives to traditional health care delivery, such as health maintenance organizations (HMOs) and preferred provider organizations (PPOs).

This resulted in unprecedented declines in hospital admissions, and patients reduced the length of their stays in hospitals as well. Hospitals were forced to modify their cost structures and the types of products and services offered. The once-calm hospital supply industry became extremely volatile, now being constrained by the new, strict Medicare reimbursement rules; the emergence of "less invasive" surgical techniques; insurance coverage that places a greater burden of payment on the patient, and competition from health maintenance organizations, specialized care centers, and home health care. In 1984 Baxter's earnings dropped 87 percent from the year before, to a meager $29 million.

Rival hospital suppliers like Abbott Laboratories, Becton Dickinson, and C. R. Bard began to compete fiercely on price. Smelling blood, Abbott launched a price war in intravenous solutions, Baxter's most important product line. That struggle ended with market shares unchanged—48 percent for Baxter, 42 percent for Abbott. However, prices were now 30 percent lower for all products in this area.

Reorientation

Loucks had spent the majority of his corporate career at Baxter. In 1984, he had come to believe that with a continued concentration in areas such as intravenous systems, blood products, and dialysis, the firm would remain at a permanent disadvantage due to its narrow product line and poor distribution system. Abbott Laboratories and Johnson & Johnson had many more high-margin products than Baxter. Loucks knew that while Abbott boasted a return on equity of 31.7 percent and margins of 14.5 percent, Baxter lagged, with a 14.1 percent return on equity and a thin, 5.4 percent operating margin. Consequently, Loucks believed that he had to formulate a new strategy.

The new strategy called for Baxter to become a full-service provider to hospitals and to diversify by moving from being a hospital supplier to actually becoming a health care provider. Moreover, the firm began to supply new services to hospitals, management consulting, and computer services to help administrators struggling with the medical economics of the 1980s.

In 1985, chairman of American Hospital Supply (AHS) Karl Bays launched an attempt to merge with hospital-management giant HCA (later HCA Healthcare) for $36 a share. Wall Street refused to believe that there was synergy between the two companies, but Loucks saw an opportunity and tendered a $51 per share bid for AHS. After a fierce, three-week struggle, AHS fell to the much smaller Baxter for the purchase price of $3.7 billion. Analysts at the time believed that the companies would have important areas of strategic fit, such as Baxter's ability to move its popular intravenous solutions and blood products through American Hospital's superior marketing and distribution systems. In addition, these firms had few overlapping products but shared many of the same customers. It appeared that the combined companies could significantly reduce costs by consolidating their sales, manufacturing, marketing, and management functions.

The acquisition of AHS allowed Baxter to become a full-service provider to hospitals. The new Baxter now possessed a product line that covered about 70 percent of a hospital's supply needs—everything from scalpels to intravenous solutions. Baxter believed that this would be attractive to hospitals wishing to cut overhead expenses by dealing with fewer suppliers. Loucks planned to bundle the company's traditional products—intravenous, blood therapy, hemodialysis, and urological products—with new services, such as cost consulting, that can save money and improve productivity for hospitals. Loucks argued at the time, "With this one step we played into the strength of where the market is moving—namely, toward suppliers who offer the broadest array of merchandise and services" (Rublin 1991, 20). AHS, whose 1984 sales were $3.4 billion (double Baxter's sales), certainly fit that description. The company was known for its huge product assortment (most of it, however, manufactured by other firms), and its state-of-the-art domestic distribution network. Baxter's competitive advantage was its manufacturing and technological expertise, which were focused on a narrower product line.

To accomplish the merger Baxter had to take on a staggering $2 billion in debt to finance part of the purchase. The company also issued approximately 80 million new shares. Baxter's management completed a comprehensive review of the new organization's businesses to determine which could be sold to reduce the debt load. The result was that five of its operations were spun off to shareholders. Loucks used a major chunk of the $1.2 billion proceeds from these sales to pay down Baxter's debt.

Management also decided to reorganize the structure of the organization, which was streamlined by reducing the layers of management and consolidating the current ten operating units into only five: hospital operations, sales/distribution, alternate site services, special businesses (diagnostics, blood therapy, and surgical/critical-care products), and the World Trade Group (international operations). This was intended to refocus the company to more closely mirror the way the hospitals were now making their purchases. In addition, the company reduced its workforce by about 5,000.

Loucks also emphasized diversification to meet the changing nature of health care. He saw that hospitals were shifting more patients to alternate sites such as "doc in a box" surgical centers and home care. Suppliers of these services were enjoying more liberal reimbursement rates. In 1986, Baxter moved into these new, fast-growing markets as well. In 1987, Baxter spent $550 million to buy Caremark, the largest alternate-site outpatient-care player.

Results: Too Many New Businesses

Not surprisingly, with a merger of such large companies, complications arose. Perhaps the most difficult problem, after financing, was the merging of two very different cultures. One indicator of the problem was the continuing shake-up of the top management team. Three former top-level AHS executives left the company soon after the takeover was completed. The highest-ranking executive was Frank A. Ehmann, who had been AHS's president. Karl D. Bays, a divisional chief executive, had his responsibilities reduced. He was still Baxter's chairman but retained no operating authority. Bays left in 1987 to become chief executive of IC Industries. Loucks explained that the reason for the shake-up was management's disagreement over the strategy changes (Deveny 1986).

As Baxter entered the 1990s, profits continued to be less than the industry average. After the merger and four years of almost continuous restructuring and cost cutting, Baxter was still essentially a high-volume distributor of low-margin products.The firm was generating only a 6 percent net profit margin and 10 percent return on equity, compared with the 15 percent margin and 30 percent return enjoyed by Abbott. Abbott was big in nutritional products and sophisticated diagnostic equipment, products which typically enjoyed gross margins that exceeded 40 percent.

In response, in 1990 Loucks announced a decision, to launch the biggest restructuring in its fifty-nine-year history. First, he revamped the manufacturing systems to improve productivity and quality. In addition, he consolidated twenty-one manufacturing facilities worldwide and decentralized corporate staff positions. In total the company eliminated 6,400 employees. Second, he fine-tuned the corporate strategy. Baxter spun off part of its $1.4 billion diagnostics business. Loucks wanted to develop new products and services with higher margins (higher technology) and to more aggressively expand Baxter's sales in international markets (Flynn 1990). The cost of this restructuring was $566 million.

As a result of continuing poor performance, Loucks and his management team decided that the firm lacked sufficient strategic focus and that the patient care division was a drain on the firm's resources. As a result, in 1992 the decision was made to spin off Caremark to Baxter's shareholders. Baxter would return to being only a supplier to hospitals, and not a provider of patient care. Loucks also announced a $2 billion expansion effort to develop business in the Far East and South America.

The situation worsened in 1993, when Baxter reported a loss from continuing operations of $288 million on sales of $8.9 billion; this amounted to a return on equity of negative 7.7 percent. Many investors were openly calling for Loucks's removal. The stock price hit a low of $22 per share, down from $40 in 1991. Investors began calling for the company to be split in two; one firm would continue to sell low-margin medical supplies (such as gowns and surgical trays) and the other would sell Baxter's lucrative medical specialty products.

Loucks did not want to abandon his existing strategy. Instead, he requested that all top managers borrow twice their annual salary to purchase Baxter stock. In addition, sixty-three of the firm's top managers took out personal loans to purchase $121 million in company stock. Loucks cut the number of employees and management an additional 5 percent and radically altered the sales force. Moreover, he slashed inventory costs by installing a new information system to better coordinate shipments to big customers.

In 1994, Baxter completed the sale of its diagnostic business. Loucks also announced a change in an important corporate-wide control system—management compensation. In the past, management's compensation had been tied to earnings. Now, however, it became tied to shareholder value. Baxter would pay its management based on the firm's financial performance relative to the Standard & Poor's Medical Products and Supplies Index.

Finally, in 1995, Loucks accepted that his current strategy had not been effective. He announced that he would bow to the desires of shareholders and divide the company into two separate operations. This separation would provide both firms the ability to have a clearer focus, and there were to be fewer tradeoffs. The first business would be called Allegiance Corporation, it would consist of the low-margin health care products and the health care cost-management service operations. This multibillion-dollar business was to be spun off to shareholders and listed on the New York Stock Exchange. The remaining businesses would be kept under the Baxter name, and the firm would renew its focus on its core technologies, which included renal technology, biotechnology, cardiovascular medicine, and medication delivery. Loucks reported that the new Baxter would spend $700 million a year on research and development, which was twice as much as was spent in 1990. By the end of the year, Baxter's stock price had more than doubled, to $48. The return to stockholders equity in 1995 was 18.5 percent, and in 1996 it was 24.3 percent.

By the end of 1989, Loucks had succeeded in implementing the strategy he had formulated in 1985. As a result of the merger and diversification programs, only 15 percent of Baxter's sales remained in the original core business of sterile fluids, compared to more than 60 percent of sales in 1984. This represented a massive shift in the product mix for a company of Baxter's size. This strategy of moving to higher margin, higher technology products was important and necessary to the firm. However, if we use the standard of an average industry return to shareholders, then Loucks was unsuccessful.

The 1995 announcement that the company would be split into two separate firms was Louck's admission that the original strategy of diversification was not going to work. The firm was not able to diversify successfully into the health care management field or improve its position in its traditional medical products. Many of the products that came with AHS were low-tech, low-margin products, which further hurt Baxter's overall corporate performance. Management divided its attention, and the firm's resources were inadequate to successfully compete in these industries. If Loucks had had the advantage of hindsight, he would have known that the two purchases that Baxter made (American Hospital Supply and Caremark) increased its exposure to the very markets that would soon come under the most cost-cutting pressure from hospitals and the federal government.

In this case, speed and aggressiveness did not pay off for stockholders. Management had chosen a very risky strategy of diversifying into major new markets. Where Loucks may have failed is in his lack of one of the two keys necessary for an incumbent chief executive officer to successfully initiate a major reorientation: knowledge and experience. He diversified into new areas in which his existing executive team had little knowledge or competence. Then, as time passed and poor financial performance continued, management abandoned these efforts. As of 1997, Loucks continues to serve as the chief executive officer and chairman of the board for Baxter, positions he has held since 1980.

ROLE OF THE EXECUTIVE TEAM

The third relationship we found with regard to a firm's executive leadership was that the top management team members were generally not actively involved in initiating a reorientation. Because of the large size of the organizations we examined, we had expected that the chief executive officer would rely on key executives to carry out massive change. Many studies have found a relationship between the composition of the top management team members and the amount of major change that firms initiate (see, for example, Wiersema and Bantel 1992; Finkelstein and Hambrick 1990). Lant, Milliken, and Batra (1992) found evidence to indicate that firms that brought in new top managers were associated with reorientation.

Instead, however, we were unable to identify situations where the top management team members (excluding the chief executive officer) influenced the time taken to initiate a reorientation. Only in the case of General Mills were we able to identify the role of one member of the top management team, the chief financial officer. This executive established a new compensation program, which had a significant impact on changing the orientation of the firm's executives to focus on return to shareholders rather than just corporate growth. As a result, executives and managers began to question their long-held assumptions concerning the value of diversification.

There are two possible explanations for this result. First, the chief executive may actually be the person who is making the decision to initiate massive change. This may be logical in that the chief executive officer is the individual who has the legal authority and responsibility to direct the operations of the firm to obtain the objectives of the shareholders.

Second, the role of the top executives may be overshadowed by the chief executive's role as the key spokesperson of the firm. The top management team is likely to be involved in the strategic decision-making process as well as implementation of any new company initiatives. However, it will be the chief executive officer who reports the decisions made to the board members, press, and shareholders.

4

The Role of the Shareholders and Board of Directors

Beginning in the 1980s it became clear that a significant shift in the power of shareholders over corporate management was taking place. Some shareholders began to openly express their dissatisfaction with the returns they received from their stock investments. Large active shareholders pressured board members and executives to change organization practices in order to achieve improved returns for the shareholders. Investors called on board members to exercise their fiduciary duty to protect the interests of the firm's stockholders instead of merely serving as a rubber stamp for management decisions, as they had done for more than the last six decades.

Our research found that different types of stock owners and members of the board of directors could influence the time taken to initiate massive change. Reorientations cost so much money and change so many aspects of the organization that it stands to reason that board members and other stakeholders should be involved in some aspect of the process. At the very least, the chief executive officer will have to explain the plan to the board of directors.

However, the ways in which the shareholders and board members affected the process turned out to be very different. Firm managers who are stock owners (inside owners), institutional owners, large shareholders, and different types of board directors all had certain roles, and almost all of these roles are changing as the decade of the 1990s draws to a close.

THE SEPARATION OF OWNERSHIP FROM CONTROL

Adolph Berle and Gardiner Means, in their 1932 landmark book, *The Modern Corporation and Private Property,* were the first to identify the shift of power away from the founding families (shareholders) of large corporations to professional managers. The owner-managers of the large corporations of the nineteenth century were being replaced by thousands of individual investors who had no long-term interest in the firm. One study reported that by 1974, 82 percent of the country's largest corporations had come under management control (Useem 1993). As Alfred Chandler reported in *The Invisible Hand* (1977), in general, the founding families had relinquished all but residual control over company decisions.

By law, individual stockholders had legal control over U.S. corporations. However, they did not have effective control. It was too expensive for the thousands, or possibly millions, of individual shareholders to try to influence a firm's management. The single shareholder whose investment was limited had neither the incentive nor the ability to gather information and monitor the activities of the firm's management. Instead, if an individual shareholder was dissatisfied with the firm's performance, it was easier and quicker just to sell the shares and invest the money elsewhere.

The result is that professional managers became accountable to no one and were able to pursue their own interests, which might or might not be the same as their shareholders. Many observers of corporate behavior would say that most boards of directors have become dominated by firm managers. The chief executive officer, who is very often also the chairperson of the board, controls the solicitation and voting of proxies. In addition, this person controls the board's internal operation nominating all committee chairpersons and assigning duties to board members. The result is that the board of directors has become little more than a rubber stamp for management decisions. Under these circumstances, it is expected that managers will pursue strategies that increase their own compensation, power, and security.

Agency theory examines the relationship between those who bear the risk (shareholders) and the agents they hire to manage it (managers). Agency theorists argue that there is a conflict of interest between shareholders and managers. The shareholders are primarily concerned with achieving improvement in the value of their investment. On the other hand, the managers' primary concern is with the firm's growth, which will enable them to promote employment and career advancement opportunities for themselves while providing their fellow employees with job security.

One strategy that led to growth and security for managers was diversifying a firm's products and markets to achieve a high degree of independence from the capital markets (banks and the stock market).

Frequently, managers built up slack resources such as unused debt capacity. This allowed them to avoid going to the capital markets to obtain funds since they had created their own internally available resources. This gave managers reserves on which to draw if there was an emergency or if they needed to "ride out" a period of poor financial performance. However, the diversified investors would have gotten better returns on their investments if they had been able to take those underutilized funds and invest them elsewhere.

Managers believed that if they were diversified into several different industries (unrelated diversification), then if one of the businesses was performing poorly, the other businesses would likely be performing well. This would even out the returns so that the managers could guarantee to their shareholders some level of minimal profit returns. This was thought to ensure the long-term survival of the corporate entity as well as create additional promotion opportunities and more interesting jobs for the managers themselves.

The Rise of Shareholder Power

Two major developments occurred in the 1980s that significantly shifted the power relationship that existed between a firm's management and its shareholders.

To begin with, large corporations experienced a long period of relatively poor performance in the 1970s and early 1980s. Some analysts blamed the poor performance on increasing competition caused by the integration of the world economies. However, many corporate executives blamed it on the growing role of federal regulations in social areas such as environmental protection, occupational health and safety, and equal opportunity. Instead of developing new organizational practices to overcome the long-term changes in the competitive environment, many business leaders sought a rollback in government programs.

There was a growing number of investors who believed that professional managers had been pursuing their own self-interests instead of the formers' objective, which was generating shareholder value. More and more shareholders were becoming openly dissatisfied with the financial performance of many of their stock investments. The investment community sensed that there could be a payoff, so some individual investors (often called corporate raiders), supported by financial institutions and Wall Street brokers, took action. They acquired the majority of the firm's stock, taking over decision-making control, eliminating the incumbent management, and implementing massive change in an effort to improve the value of the firm. In many cases the financial payoffs for the corporate raiders were substantial.

Since the internal governance system, made up of the existing board of directors and shareholders, had proven to be ineffective, these takeovers performed the function of providing an external control mechanism of management. Peter Drucker (1991) is one of many well-known business researchers who contended that what made the takeovers inevitable was the mediocre performance of managers who had little or no accountability to anyone.

This turnover in corporate stock ownership was enhanced by Ronald Reagan's presidential policies, which created a favorable climate for mergers or acquisitions. In 1980 there were $44 billion worth of mergers and acquisitions, and the figure reached $246.9 billion in 1988 (Useem 1993). Many of these were not friendly transactions but rather hostile takeovers.

The second development that has affected the balance of power between a firm's management and the shareholders is the growth of one class of stockholder—the institutional investors, which, by the 1990s, held over 50 percent of all available company stock in the United States. These institutional investors consist of pension funds, mutual funds, banks, and insurance companies that hold individual retirement accounts. Institutional investors have had the resources and expertise to monitor the activities of big corporations and have been obligated as a fiduciary to exercise shareholder ownership rights to protect the interests of their pension fund participants.

These two developments have caused a revolution in corporate governance. The majority of shareholders demanded that their firm's management pursue objectives that were more consistent with their investment objectives and less focused on other stakeholders. Shareholders no longer had trust in the latter groups (the managers) and instead often sought to limit their agents' discretion, over how corporate funds would be invested. Now when managers made a decision they had to determine the effect of the decision on creating shareholder value.

At the same time that institutional investors were becoming more vocal, academic researchers and many business practitioners were concluding that the managers' diversification strategies were a drag on corporate earnings. That explains why conglomerates, which had pursued unrelated diversification in the 1960s and 1970s, were the target for much of this period's hostile takeover activity. To fight off actual or potential takeover activity, firms' incumbent managers refocused their efforts on their most important core businesses and sold off underperforming divisions. This is just what the investors wanted. Managers extolled the virtues of lean operations, eliminating thousands of jobs at headquarters and delegating authority to individuals at lower levels of the organization. The consequences of the corporate restructuring of the late 1980s and early 1990s were enormous. Hundreds of thousands of people were displaced and forced to find new employment, and hundreds of thousands of others found that their jobs had been fundamentally redesigned.

Managers did not accept the rising desire of shareholders to increase their influence over the firms' strategic decisions without a fight. Management took steps to fight off this unwanted shareholder intrusion with poison pills, greenmail, and employee stock ownership plans whose stock vote they largely controlled. Furthermore, managers tried to convince the shareholders that poison pills were really for the latter group's benefit. The plans usually consisted of rights issued to shareholders that could not be used unless triggered by a takeover attempt. At that time the shareholders could purchase shares from, or sell shares back to, either the target company or the acquiring company. The plan often gave the target shareholders the chance to buy shares at up to a 50 percent discount of the acquirers' stock. Since the shareholders from the acquiring firm could not participate, they would find their own stock value reduced.

The second approach to fighting an unwanted takeover was greenmail, which was used by Phillips's management. Management offers greenmail to a large stockholder who is attempting to take over the firm, which is a bribe or payment over and above the market value of their stock to entice the stockholder to sell the shares and drop the attempt. Corporate raiders are thus given huge profits without having to take over the firm, and the entrenched managers keep their jobs. However, the firm's remaining shareholders see the value of their stock investment decline.

The third antitakeover approach is the establishment of an employee stock ownership plan (ESOP). Several companies including Polaroid, Lockheed, and Phillips Petroleum, have use ESOPs to prevent hostile takeover attempts. For ESOPs, management purchases stock from other investors and places it in trust for the firm's employees in hopes that the employees would feel a sense of ownership in the company and, more important, will become more productive so that their stock will improve in value. Thus, employee interests are more closely aligned with those of other shareholders. Company employees can acquire a substantial block of shares over a relatively short period of time. In the case of Lockheed, the ESOP is the majority stock owner.

The other impact of ESOP programs is that they put large blocks of company stock in "friendly" hands. The trustee of the ESOP (appointed by the incumbent board of directors) or the employees (if they are allowed to vote their shares) are unlikely to vote against the wishes of the incumbent executive team.

THE POWER OF INSIDE STOCKHOLDERS

Inside stock ownership refers to the amount of stock owned by the executives and managers of the firm. The percent of stock owned by executives is a measure of the power of the top management team. Agency theorists argue that as the amount of stock owned by top management team members increases, so does the alignment of interests between stockholders and managers (Fama 1980). When managers are significant stockholders, they will more likely be able to make decisions that maximize stockholder wealth (Hill and Snell 1989).

Executives who are significant stock owners theoretically should have the power to make massive change, and to do so quickly if they feel it is necessary. However, in this study, the extent of inside ownership did not influence the time the firm took to initiate a reorientation. This may be because we only examined very large corporations, in which the total market value of all stock issued is so large that managers generally will own only a relatively small amount. For the sample of firms in this research, the average total amount of outstanding stock that was held by all of the firms' executives and managers combined was only 7.3 percent. Given that the top management team in these firms can consist of more than twenty people, this level of inside ownership may be too small to align the interests of the firm's executives with shareholders. In one study it was found that managers' interests only become closely aligned with the interests of shareholders when the percentage of inside ownership reached 40 to 46 percent of total outstanding equity (Oswald and Jahera 1991).

FIVE-PERCENT SHAREHOLDERS AND CORPORATE RAIDERS

We separated large shareholders into two groups. The first group consisted of individual shareholders who own 5 percent or more of the firm's stock and have invested in the firm for more than one year. The second group was comprised of large shareholders who had purchased 5 percent of the stock but were trying to take control of the firm. These investors hold onto the firm's stock for a very short period of time (generally much less than one year), even if they succeed in taking over the firm.

Large shareholders who have invested in the firm for at least a year have an obvious personal interest in monitoring the decisions of a firm's executives in order to assure acceptable levels of long-term financial performance. These shareholders have considerable personal wealth at risk in their investment in the individual firm. They can easily get other large shareholders to align with them and together demand information from the firm's the managers to assess their performance. For these shareholders, the benefits of monitoring and evaluating managers outweigh the costs (Demsetz 1983). Chaganti and Damanpour (1991) found that these large nonmanaging shareholders were the most powerful external force affecting a firm's strategy and performance.

With such power, large stockholders could surely put pressure on management to implement major changes to the organization practices if it has been performing poorly and to force management to initiate a reorientation in less time than it otherwise might. External stakeholders are not subject to the same inertial pressures as are inside managers. A continuing crisis will provide evidence that the beliefs and practices of the existing management team are incorrect. As a result, large stockholders are likely to start questioning the effectiveness of the firm's strategies and pressure existing managers to make changes to their corporate practices (Nystrom and Starbuck 1984).

Contrary to what we expected, large long-standing shareholders were not found to have a significant effect on the time it takes a firm to initiate a reorientation. Instead, the sample firms that did reorient had 50 percent fewer large shareholders than those firms that did not. Ownership of 5 percent or more of the stock in a firm that is traded on the New York Stock Exchange represents a sizable portion of an individual or institution's wealth. These stockholders will closely monitor the strategies of firms in which they invest. However, they do not seem inclined to wait for the incumbent management to initiate a reorientation in the case of a firm experiencing poor performance. Instead they quickly sell off their stock.

Reorientations cause a disruption of internal and external relationships, and the investors cannot know how long it will take the organization to master new organizational strategies. For most of the firms in our sample that initiated a reorientation, it took at least three years before the organization was able to return to industry-average levels of performance.

Compaq Computers (discussed at the end of this chapter) is a case example in which the large shareholder had already sold his stock before the firm initiated a reorientation. Ben Rosen, the venture capitalist who was instrumental in financing the start-up of Compaq Computer, served as firm's chairman of the board of directors. By the time Compaq had found itself in a crisis during 1991, Rosen had already reduced his shareholdings in the company from 15 percent to less than 1 percent.

There was one type of large shareholder that did trigger a reorientation; the corporate raider. Corporate raiders generally purchase a large block of stock as a prelude to making public their intention to take over total control of a firm. Because the corporate raider has been an important trigger of the massive corporate change that occurred in the 1980s and 1990s, we review two case examples in this chapter: Phillips and Polaroid. These firms initiated a reorientation only after a takeover bid occurred. The reorientations were unsuccessful for the firm's shareholders, and later, the strategic direction had to be reversed.

Phillips Petroleum: Ravaged by Two Unsuccessful Takeover Attempts

In the early 1980s, worldwide oil prices continued to fall, depressing the prices of oil company stocks. Nonetheless, oil companies became takeover targets for two reasons. For one, the market value of most oil companies was lower than the appraised, or breakup, value. Second, because any new significant oil and gas discoveries in the United States are likely be in expensive-to-mine frontier areas and offshore waters, it is therefore cheaper for an oil company to replace its energy reserves by buying another oil company than by drilling.

We begin by reviewing the events that took place at Phillips Petroleum, a firm that moved very quickly to initiate a reorientation once it was faced with the threat of corporate raiders. During 1984–1985, the management of Phillips fought off two takeover attempts, from corporate raiders T. Boone Pickens and Carl Icahn.

Phillips was not prepared for the worldwide drop in oil prices. In the late 1970s, Phillips's strategy was to become an integrated global energy company. It had substantial excess current assets that had been generated from its successes in the North Sea and Alaska, which the company invested in all sorts of diversification efforts. Several analysts had argued that Phillips was wasting a lot of money in trying to become an integrated energy company (Norman 1986).

As early as 1981, however, the falling energy prices reduced the cash available for Phillips to develop further energy alternatives and mineral deposits. Phillips began planning to warehouse undeveloped mineral properties. However, the management was forced to change its strategy in 1984 when Pickens launched his attempt to acquire Phillips, closely followed by Icahn's takeover efforts.

Takeover Bids

On December 4, 1984, Pickens publicly set out to gain control of Phillips Petroleum when Mesa Partners, his investment group, announced its intention to increase its 5.7 percent stake in the company to more than 20 percent. His intention was to put up for election his own slate of board members so that he could take control of the management of the firm. Phillips stock, which had slipped below $35 a share during the summer, edged up as high as $48 on rumors of Pickens's intentions, even while worldwide crude oil prices were continuing to decline. Phillips management and Pickens filed charges and countercharges in courts from Delaware to Oklahoma all during December, with each accusing the other of having engaged in illegal activity with regard to the takeover battle.

Phillips management offered Pickens $53 a share for his stock if he would agree to go away and cease his attempt to take over the company.

Given the weakened oil market and the continuing costs of the confrontation with Phillips management, Pickens agreed to accept the offer. Pickens's Mesa Partners ended up making a pretax profit of $89 million. In addition, Phillips management agreed to reimburse Mesa for its documented "battle expenses," which were about $25 million. Obviously, for T. Boone Pickens this was not a bad return for just a few months of work (Rublin 1984). However, Wall Street investors criticized the plan as simply a greenmail payment to Pickens, made in return for his agreement to drop the takeover attempt.

To prevent future takeover attempts, Phillips management established a new employee stock ownership program, which was done to put a substantial block of stock into "friendly" hands. Phillips swapped $3.5 billion of debt securities for 58.8 million, or 38 percent, of its 154.6 million shares outstanding. The company then sold 32 million newly issued shares, for about $1.6 billion, to its new employee stock ownership plan.

The securities swap and ESOP purchase doubled the company's debt load, to around $6 billion. Accordingly, its debt-to-equity ratio increased, from about 35 to 75 percent. Once the plan was announced, Phillips stock price declined significantly. Despite the pledges of Phillips managers, the company stock sank from the $55 range to below $45 after the recapitalization plan was disclosed. Some Wall Street analysts predicted that once the company was well-insulated from any more takeover threats, the debt-heavy Phillips stocks could drop back to around $35 (Norman 1985).

Before this agreement between Phillips and the Mesa group (reached late in December 1984) could be submitted for stockholder approval (at a special meeting in February 1985), a second unfriendly effort to acquire control of the company was initiated by an investor group headed by Carl C. Icahn. Operating separately from Pickens but with a common purpose, Wall Street financiers Carl Icahn and Ivan Boesky bought 10 percent of Phillips's shares. These investors stated that they adamantly opposed the Phillips recapitalization plan, which was scheduled for a shareholders' vote on February 22. Their object was to pressure Phillips management into sweetening the restructuring offer. They also hoped that their actions might draw out one of the other big oil companies that was rumored to be investigating the possible purchase of Phillips—Atlantic Richfield, Standard Oil (Ohio), Standard Oil (Indiana), Diamond Shamrock, or Pennzoil. Institutional investors, who held almost half the Phillips stock, were expected to support the management restructuring offer unless a better deal came along.

This second tender offer was also defeated, and the shareholders voted for the recapitalization plan that had been developed to fight off the Pickens tender offer. However, the proposal failed to win the necessary majority of all outstanding shares, and it became apparent that many shareholders were interested in a different type of transaction. Consequently, on March 4, Phillips management offered to exchange a package of debt securities for approximately 50 percent of the outstanding stock. In addition, for $1.6 billion, Phillips purchased Aminoil Inc., the energy subsidiary of R. J. Reynolds. This acquisition added significantly to the company's petroleum reserves.

As a consequence of these actions, the acquisition and the return to the company's shareholders of approximately $4.5 billion in equity, Phillips's debt levels reached $8.6 billion. In addition, when the chief executive officer reached normal retirement age, the board of directors named a new chairman and chief executive officer, C. J. Silas. Silas had been with Phillips for a number of years and had participated in developing the steps that were taken to fight off the takeover attempts.

Silas, in his 1985 letter to Phillips shareholders, reaffirmed that the board of directors had determined that these takeover attempts had treated them unfairly. He contended that these attacks could have resulted in the liquidation of Phillips at "fire sale" prices, and so the board had rejected the Pickens and Icahn offers and come up with its own plan. He also pointed out that the big gainers were Pickens and Icahn. Silas claimed that Pickens had made more than $4 million a day for his raid on Phillips and Icahn had pocketed $40 to $60 million in pretax profit. He admitted that to prevent hostile raids, Phillips had been forced to sacrifice its long-term objectives for immediate, higher payouts to shareholders. He also argued that Phillips had become a "stronger and wiser" company.

Reorientation

After the two back-to-back takeover attempts, it was clear that Phillips no longer had the luxury of trying to become an integrated global energy company. As a matter of fact, given the debt levels, a reorientation was necessary to ensure the firm's very survival. Management's only real choice was to concentrate on Phillips's basic business: oil and gas. The company shifted its emphasis to developing domestic discoveries rather than continue international exploration, and Silas stated that Phillips would now become a fully integrated domestic oil company with sizable reserves in the North Sea.

The company reorganized, eliminating major divisions and cutting employment from 38,000 to less that 24,000, almost a 30 percent reduction in the total workforce. Silas slashed capital spending from $2 billion to $600 million, and the firm sold off about $2 billion of some of its most valuable assets. In 1986, Phillips sold some of its refining and marketing operations and its chemicals division. The proceeds were used to pay down the debt.

Silas instituted a new corporate culture. The personnel cutbacks ousted many of the long-tenured employees, leaving a much younger organization. Freewheeling spending was out, and strict cost controls were in effect. All company actions had to pass rigorous profit and cash criteria before being approved (Norman 1986).

A Long Recovery, a Lingering Takeover Threat

By 1987 Phillips had still not recovered from its Pyrrhic victory against the takeover attempts. Phillips's financial performance continued to be poor. Debt levels still stood at $5.7 billion, interest charges exceeded $700 million annually. Phillips's net income fell from $810 million in 1984 to $418 million in 1985 and $288 million in 1986. In the first nine months of 1987, Phillips was only able to show earnings of $2 million on $7 billion of revenue (Meyer 1988).

Only in 1988 did Phillips achieve a significant turnaround in its financial results. The downstream operations—chemicals and refining—turned in an outstanding performance, generating $1.13 billion in cash, which enabled Philips to make a $900 million payment on its debt. As a result, the company's average yearly payments dropped to a manageable $332 million. Even corporate raider Pickens was impressed with what Silas had been able to accomplish. Phillips's success was all the more remarkable given the current low oil prices. Phillips's strategy of being very selective in choosing potential exploration sites resulted in the percentage of dry holes drilled declining to 45 in 1988, down from 73 percent in 1986.

That same year, however, Wall Street analysts were again identifying Phillips as one of the top takeover candidates of 1988. Because its debt levels remained high, it had virtually no financial maneuvering room. As a result, the company was a sitting duck for anyone who could afford to make a $3 billion takeover bid and had the patience to wait for those assets to become salable once the oil market had improved. Several analysts predicted that Phillips would not pay down its debt too far because it wanted to ward off any new takeover attempts. Its stock price was trading at nearly $20, up 39 percent from year-end 1987. However, this still represented only 60 percent of Phillips's appraised value.

Silas was taking no chances. He announced at the April 1988 shareholders meeting that Phillips had adopted provisions to outlaw shareholder-called meetings and restrict bylaw amendments. He also increased the employee stock ownership plan, which already held 20 percent of the company's stock for the employees.

Phillips continued to experience erratic performance. Despite higher worldwide oil prices in 1989, its downstream businesses performed poorly, even though debt was reduced by $869 million. Net income rose to

$719 million in 1990 (versus $219 million in 1989). Earnings only ranged from $180 million to $268 million in 1991 through 1993.

In 1994, Silas retired and another long-serving Phillips executive, Wayne Allen, became his successor. Allen announced a structural reorganization, and the company was split into two units. Management created a new chemical division with revenues of $2.3 billion to emphasize the importance of the chemical business. However, many analysts expected that the chemical company would be spun off to stockholders because the business had been generating negative earnings. The other unit contained Phillips's traditional oil and gas business. Allen also instituted a new measure to be used to evaluate all capital-spending projects: economic value added. This measure (defined as net after-tax profit less the cost of capital) is considered to be a more accurate indicator of the effect of management decisions on shareholder value.

In 1996, Phillips was able to report that in the last three years it had made above average-industry returns to shareholders. The economic value added had increased by 53 percent since 1993, and the return to shareholders in 1996 was 28 percent. Allen reaffirmed Phillips's commitment to remain independent. He stated in his *1996 Letter to Shareholders* that Phillips had always been "fiercely independent" and would continue to stay that way.

In 1996 and 1997, the oil industry went through a new stage of consolidation. After years of downsizing, spinning off nonenergy operations, and restructuring, oil firms were now turning again to mergers and acquisitions. As a result of low debt levels and fierce competition for new reserves, firms decided it was cheaper to purchase existing reserves. In 1996, the oil industry had completed $28.3 billion of mergers and acquisitions, and in June 1997, the level of activity had already exceeded $20 billion.

The Phillips management should have realized in the early 1980s that the environment was changing and their strategy to become a fully integrated global energy company was no longer valid. The efforts of Pickens and Icahn forced management to abandon that strategy, regardless of its own objectives and desires. Managers were very slow to initiate reorientation and only did so when they were forced to on threat of losing their jobs. To maintain their independence, the managers paid the corporate raiders part of Phillips stockholder equity, which was not available to other shareholders. They undertook a debt load that seriously raised the risks that the firm would default and reduced its ability to succeed in the future. Interestingly, even in 1996, Phillips management continues to signal corporate raiders that their intention is to maintain managerial independence.

Polaroid: Unsuccessful Takeover Attempt and Reorientation

A Snapshot of the Polaroid Experience

Polaroid is another example of a firm in which corporate raiders affected the timing of a reorientation. Incumbent management only initiated the reorientation in an attempt to fight off a takeover attempt.

In the 1980s, this firm was experiencing a loss in direction as a result of the retirement of its charismatic founder, Edwin H. Land. In addition, Polaroid's financial performance was below the industry average. Substantial amounts of money were being invested in research and development, but management had little to show for its efforts.

Shamrock Holdings saw an opportunity to earn substantial profits by taking over Polaroid and implementing a new strategic direction. The actions that the Polaroid management took to avoid a loss of decision-making control appear to be a classic example of management's concern for its own welfare above the interests of the shareholders. The reorientation that the entrenched management implemented at the time of the takeover bid was successful in preventing the takeover but never proved financially successful for the shareholders. After experiencing a profit loss in 1995, the board finally took action by appointing the first outside chief executive officer in the history of the firm.

Setting the Stage

Land founded a very successful business and company culture based on creating markets through scientific invention. However, once the technical miracles ended (in the 1980s), Polaroid found itself unequipped to continue developing new products to meet consumer demands. More and more consumers favored the use of 35 millimeter (mm) cameras, which produced better-quality prints than Polaroid and cost half as much as the latter's instant prints.

The culture that Land had created at Polaroid was characterized as being paternalistic, possessing expensive personnel policies, and having limited manufacturing flexibility and slow decision making. Once Land left the company, the firm's research organization, lacking his charismatic leadership, lost direction. Land had previously made all the firm's decisions and provided all the strategic direction (Hammonds 1988).

Though Polaroid was responsible for developing instant-imaging technology, the company faced heavy competition from the increasingly cheaper, high-quality 35mm cameras. In the late 1980s, Polaroid was experiencing low profits but had a potentially enormous asset in the form of a patent infringement suit against Kodak, which was expected to bring up to $6 billion. The existing management team, most of whom had spent their entire careers at Polaroid, continued to downsize the corporation and look for new markets and products.

Incumbent management dramatically cut the workforce through expensive early-retirement and other buyout programs. From 1979 to 1987, the total number of people employed at Polaroid had dropped from 20,000 to around 11,000, but productivity per employee remained unchanged. During this same time frame, at two competitors, Kodak and 3M, productivity per employee had doubled. In addition, Polaroid's attempts to diversify outside film had produced poor results. For example, its move into disk drives was a catastrophe (Wrubel 1989).

Not only were these initiatives unsuccessful, they also diverted management attention. In Polaroid's core market, instant amateur photography, market share had declined from 29 percent of the total U.S. camera market in 1978 to just 14 percent in 1989. Revenues began to fall and profits plummeted, yet the individuals responsible for governance of Polaroid failed to take action. In four years, from 1984 to 1988, unit sales of instant film (on which Polaroid makes most of its money) declined an estimated 15 percent. The board of directors, whose membership had changed only slightly in the past fifteen years, took no action to try to force the firm's executives to develop a clear strategic direction.

Shamrock Holdings: The Corporate Raider

In 1978, Roy Disney quit the Walt Disney Company after disputes with management about how to revitalize the deteriorating Disney studios. Roy realized that he was likely to become impoverished when he witnessed the value of his Disney stock dwindle from $80 million to $45 million in six months. He and his wife contributed $2 million of their own money and borrowed against the Disney stock they owned to create an investment company, Shamrock Holdings, for themselves and their four children.

Roy Disney was able to parlay this initial $2 million investment into an asset pool of some $700 million, which equated to an annual compound growth rate of 70 percent. Shamrock Holdings became a formidable investment vehicle with diversified holdings in real estate, broadcasting, retailing, and oil-field construction equipment. Shamrock focused on creating long-term value in the companies in which it invested. When it identified an investment, it usually made a friendly offer for a controlling interest in the company. Stanley Gold, the chief executive officer of Shamrock Holdings, explained, "We buy companies, build them, have fun, and make a lot of money" (Rice 1989, 162). Shamrock did not like to be involved in hostile takeovers.

The Bid for Polaroid

On June 16, 1988, Stanley Gold tried to reach Polaroid's CEO, MacAllister Booth, by phone to request a meeting. Booth said he was unavailable and immediately set up a meeting with representatives of Shearson Lehman Brothers, Polaroid's investment bankers, to develop a plan to resist the expected takeover attempt. Gold continued to try to set up a meeting with Booth, who finally agreed to meet on July 13; however, the meeting never took place. On July 12, a special Polaroid board meeting was held to approve a comprehensive plan to reorganize the company. Included in the plan was the establishment of an employee stock ownership plan (ESOP) that would hold 14 percent of Polaroid's stock. Under Delaware law, a hostile acquirer must gain 85 percent of a company's shares to consummate a merger within three years. If Polaroid was able to put 14 percent of its shares in the hands of its employees, Shamrock's bid would surely fail because the employees would vote with management in opposition to the takeover bid.

Booth proposed to fund the ESOP through three approaches. First, employees would accept a 5 percent reduction in take-home pay and officers, a 10 percent reduction. Second, money matched by the firm for employees who put money into the (401k) savings plan would be used to pay off the ESOP. Finally, the normal annual pay increases of up to 5 percent would be reduced. In 1989 the increase was going to be 2 percent. With the 5 percent reduction in take-home pay and the 3 percent reduction in raises, in 1989 every employee would receive 8 percent less than had there been no ESOP.

I. M. Booth claimed that the purpose of the ESOP was to encourage employees to have the same interests in their work as stock owners.

And we believed that through ownership they would feel the importance of improving earnings and not just of their wages. So if improving the earnings and the stock price of a company is in the best interest of the shareholders, and therefore some dissident shareholder doesn't think he can come in and do it better—if that's called "anti-takeover" then I would agree that what we put in was an anti-takeover measure. (Picker 1989, 87)

In September Shamrock bid $42 for all the outstanding shares, contingent on 90 percent of all shares being tendered. Gold announced Shamrock's strategy for Polaroid to turn the business around. Polaroid would concentrate on the core business—the manufacture and sale of instant film—nothing more and nothing less. Gold believed that Polaroid's management had been spending too much time and effort in areas where the firm did not belong. He would stop Polaroid's efforts in the 35mm film market, increase marketing, give away cameras in order to sell film, and license camera technology to anyone. In addition, Gold would greatly expand international sales, especially to China, India, and the Soviet Union.

As Gold explained about Polaroid: "They are not a camera company. They make cameras at best at break-even. They are not a high-tech company. They are an old-tech company with a single elegant technology. They are in the business of selling instant film. That's where the margins are, and that's what this management can't do well" (Wrubel 1989, 66).

Shamrock bitterly protested the actions that Polaroid's board took to prevent the takeover, arguing that these steps would not improve shareholder value and sought to have the ESOP invalidated in the Delaware courts, arguing that the Polaroid board had breached its fiduciary responsibilities. Shamrock argued that the ESOP was created solely to defeat a potential takeover bid. In Delaware, the actions of corporate management are seldom overturned. The court only rules against corporate management if it has violated the so-called business judgment rule in taking the action. This requires the complaining party to prove gross negligence, which is extremely difficult. However, the court uses a higher standard to judge the actions taken by a firm's management in response to a takeover threat because of the strong possibility of a conflict of interest.

The presiding judge ruled that Polaroid's board had acted hastily by reaching its decision in only two hours with no materials having been distributed before the meeting (Monks and Minow 1995). Further, the court decided that Polaroid's ESOP was installed primarily for defensive purposes but that it adoption did not hurt Polaroid shareholders. The court ruled that ESOPs generally increase productivity and that the plan's after-tax cost was offset by the pay reductions (Rice 1989). Shamrock appealed the ruling to the Delaware Supreme Court.

In addition to the ESOP, on January 30, 1989, Polaroid announced a $1.125 billion common stock repurchase program for 24.5 million of its outstanding shares at an average price of about $46. This would reduce Polaroid's outstanding shares by 34 percent and leave the ESOP controlling over 20 percent of the shares. Polaroid issued $300 million of preferred shares to Corporate Partners, a $1.5 billion fund managed by Lazard Freres, which granted the fund about 10 percent vote. The effect of these steps was to place nearly 30 percent of the voting stock in friendly hands, which virtually guaranteed the current management continued employment despite the poor financial results it had been generating for shareholders.

Management Victory, Shareholder Loss

As a result of these steps it became impossible for Shamrock Holdings to win the proxy battle at the annual meeting. However, before it came to a vote, a settlement was reached between Shamrock and Polaroid wherein Polaroid agreed to repay the expenses that Shamrock had incurred in the takeover attempt ($20 million) and to purchase $5 million in advertising space on Shamrock's radio and TV stations. Shamrock agreed not to seek control of Polaroid for ten years. Without Shamrock's bid holding up the price of the stock, the share price fell. "It's definitely a raw deal for institutional and individual investors," said Alex Henderson of Prudential-Bache. "The ESOP and Corporate Partners made out like bandits. Those deals took money out of the company to help keep management in their jobs" (Wrubel 1989, 66). No one could disagree with Stanley Gold's comment: "Tell me these deals are for the economic benefit of the company. They sell 10 million shares to an ESOP at $31 and buy 10 million shares back at $50 in the tender. That's a pure old-fashioned loss of $190 million" (Wrubel 1989, 66).

Reorientation

By this time, Polaroid's management could no longer avoid implementing a reorientation. By the end of the takeover battle, in 1989, the company's head count had been cut to 11,400, down from 14,700.

Polaroid was going to stop thinking of itself as simply an instant photography firm. As stated in the *1988 Letter to Stockholders,* "We at Polaroid share a clear vision of the Company's future as a worldwide leader in imaging, moving beyond the boundaries of our history as an instant camera company to serve a broad spectrum of the rapidly growing and changing image recording marketplace of the future with a broad complement of imaging systems—instant, conventional and electronic."

By targeting the entire imaging industry—from photocopying to printing and video as well as photography—Polaroid saw a chance to compete in a rapidly growing, $150 billion global business. The strategy was to focus on three areas: (1) expanding consumer, business, and industrial use of instant photography; (2) capitalizing on its brand name in videotape and conventional film; and (3) developing a wide variety of products in the field of electronic imaging.

Also in 1988, the firm restructured itsinielf into three separate business units. It was now organized around three market-oriented groups, each with a worldwide focus: Family Imaging, Business Imaging, and Technical and Industrial Imaging. Management also created a separate Electronic Imaging group, which was responsible for identifying new business opportunities and supporting the imaging needs of customers in each of the market-oriented groups. The intent was to force managers to more clearly focus on meeting the needs of different groups of customers.

A new, corporate-wide, total quality and ownership program was another dimension of this reorientation. "We have found new ways of working together which produce more and better products with 15 percent fewer people in the workforce. A new compensation system, soon to be operational, will further reward employees for developing new skills and adding to their responsibilities" stated the *1989 Letter to Shareholders.*

The plan included in-house training and education programs, an employee stock ownership program, and an extensive work- redesign effort.

Aftermath: Lack of Success

What was the effect of Polaroid managers' attempts to maintain their independence? Shamrock had offered shareholders $45 per share in 1988. In 1991, the stock was selling for $25 (Palmer 1991). Polaroid continued to experience a long-term decline in instant-camera sales, and the stock market was uncertain about the potential of the firm's announced new products. Booth, who was still Polaroid's president and chief executive officer in 1990, stated that the reorganization that the firm underwent in 1989 had made Polaroid a better-managed company. But as Booth admitted, it was taking them a lot longer than expected to obtain acceptable financial returns, and he warned shareholders that 1991 and 1992 would not be any better.

The only bright spot was Polaroid's settlement with Kodak of its fourteen-year patent infringement lawsuit. A Boston court ordered Kodak to pay Polaroid $985 million, or $19.75 a share, an amount equal to all of Polaroid's operating earnings from 1985 through 1990. However, much of this extraordinary gain had to be spent strengthening the balance sheet by paying off the debt that had resulted from management's efforts to fight the Shamrock takeover bid. Booth used about $160 million of the settlement to retire long-term debt and $280 million (plus $140 million worth of convertible debentures) to retire preferred stock held by Corporate Partners L.P., the affiliate of the investment banking firm Lazard Freres that had helped rescue Polaroid from Shamrock. An additional $150 million was used to buy back company stock.

Polaroid's performance continued to be erratic, with net income in 1993 declining 33 percent, to only $67.9 million. Booth then reported that he would accelerate Polaroid's move into electronic imaging. His goal was to reach $42 billion in sales of electronics products by the year 2000. He explained that there were many more opportunities than just those in instant photography, which at this time still accounted for 85 percent of total corporate sales. As a result, Polaroid continued to deemphasize the areas it knew best and to push into highly competitive new markets in which it had yet to develop any significant new, successful products.

Finally, an Outside Successor

In 1995 Polaroid showed an operating loss of $140 million and the board finally took action, appointing a new chief executive officer, Gary DiCamillo. DiCamillo was the first outside manager to lead the camera maker in its fifty-five-year history. DiCamillo was forty-four-years old and the number two executive at Black and Decker; he was given credit for building up that power tools business.

As soon as DiCamillo arrived at Polaroid, he announced another major reorientation. The firm would reemphasize its instant photography business, especially in North America, Japan, and Western Europe. DiCamillo launched Polaroid's first large-scale advertising campaign in more than a decade. Even after all Booth's efforts to diversify Polaroid, instant photography still accounted for 90 percent of sales. The second element of the reorientation was that the firm was reorganized around three different core areas than under Booth: Consumer, Commercial, and New Business. Third, he introduced a new performance and incentive system based on improvement in economic value added. DiCamillo hoped that economic value added (the same measure used by Allen at Phillips) would more closely align management interests with shareholders.

DiCamillo brought eight new officers and more than twenty other outside executives into the company. These executives had extensive experience in successfully bringing new products to the market. They came from other industries, such as GE, Nabisco, and Kraft Foods. Polaroid's net income for 1996 was reported to be $202 million. In just one year, DiCamillo had done what Booth could not accomplish in a decade.

This is another example of a firm in which the incumbent managers were slow to initiate a reorientation. They only did so when faced with the prospect of losing their jobs, yet in the end, many of them lost their jobs anyway. Moreover, as in the case of Phillips Petroleum, the strategic direction that was chosen was unrealistic and the reorientation was poorly executed. The corporate strategy of product and market diversification that this entrenched management instituted failed to produce any improvement in Polaroid's financial position.

Interestingly, the new strategic orientation that DiCamillo implemented is basically the same strategy that Shamrock Holdings would have implemented had their takeover bid been successful. We speculate that had Shamrock been able to acquire Polaroid back in 1989, the shareholders would have probably seen a much better return on their investment in Polaroid stock.

Polaroid's antitakeover strategy became the model for other corporations' incumbent managers when fighting unsolicited takeovers. Some eighty corporations established or enlarged their own ESOPs in 1989 (Bruner and Brownlee 1990).

INSTITUTIONAL INVESTORS

Perhaps the most important trend in corporate governance today is the growing ownership position of institutional investors in major U.S.

corporations. Institutional owners are radically different shareholders from the dedicated individual investor. Institutional fund managers can move across the full range of corporate equities throughout the world. They are extremely mobile and highly diversified, and their only concern is improving portfolio performance.

In 1950, institutional investors accounted for only about 12 percent of all shares on New York Stock Exchange (Taylor 1990), but by 1992, institutions controlled an estimated $8.3 trillion worth of corporate assets and accounted for more than 47 percent of all outstanding equities (Brancato 1993). Much of this astounding growth in institutional ownership has resulted from the expansion of pension funds, which, by the year 2000, are expected to hold 50 percent of all corporate equity (Nussbaum and Dobrzynski 1987). Clearly, the growing influence of the institutional owner should be of utmost interest to academic researchers and corporate management.

After 1945, the federal government provided substantial tax incentives for individuals and employers to encourage employees to save for their retirement. This program was very successful and transferred a substantial amount of national savings from savings accounts in banks to pension plans. Individual taxpayers responded to the tax incentives, preferring to have one dollar in their pension plan rather than seventy cents in their savings account at the bank (Monks and Minow 1996). The result is that the largest amount of investment capital in the world is held by institutional investors.

The popular press has reported that many chief executive officers have been pressured by institutional investors to alter their firms' corporate strategies. For example, Sears, Roebuck & Company's management was forced to divest its financial businesses (Star 1993). In many of these events, it is the institutional investor that has played the pivotal role in pressuring the firm's management to change its corporate direction.

Some observers of the governance process believe that institutional investors have used their increasing influence to pressure management for short-term gains. Many of these investors, especially managers of mutual funds, face tremendous pressure from their individual clients to generate high quarterly performance results.

An early example of the potential power of institutional investors on corporations occurred at General Motors. The California Public Employees Retirement System (CalPERS), which held a large amount of General Motors stock, questioned General Motors's CEO succession process (Monks and Minow 1995). More generally, many of the nation's best-known chief executive officers complain that institutional investors pressure executives to show short-term profits (Nussbaum and Dobrzynski 1987).

The question of whether institutional investors are using their growing influence to force firms to pursue strategies that affect short-term or long-term outcomes is still largely unanswered. The research that specifically addresses this issue has found mixed results. Several studies have found evidence to indicate that institutional investors have used their increasing influence to pressure management to focus on short-term results (Graves 1988; Hansen and Hill 1991). Others have found that active institutional owners are associated with firms that pursue investments in research and development, which have a positive long-term effect on firm performance (Jarrell, Lehn, and Marr 1985; Baysinger, Kosnick, and Turk 1991).

Many observers of corporate governance have argued that in the past, institutional investors followed the "Wall Street Rule" (Useem 1993; Monks and Minow 1995): they either voted with the management of the firms in which they held stock or, if they disagreed with management, sold their stock.

We found that the actions of institutional investors did not affect the time taken to initiate a reorientation. Indeed, in our entire analysis, institutional investors failed to have a significant impact on the time taken to initiate a reorientation. This result is consistent with other research conducted in this area (see, for example, Bethel and Liebeskind 1993; Grinyer, Mayes, and McKiernan 1988).

Our results indicate that institutional investors do not normally get actively involved with the management of the firms in which they invest. There are two possible explanations for this result. The first is that institutional investors tend to have such a diversified portfolio that they cannot effectively monitor any single firm (Lowenstein 1991). In addition, it may be that they are not as big a force as they are made out to be. Perhaps many institutions own a relatively small amount of each firm's shares and so cannot exercise the same voting power as shareholders who own 5 percent or more of the shares of a single firm.

The second explanation is that institutional investors are not one homogeneous group. Institutional investors include mutual funds, insurance companies, public and private pension funds, endowment funds, and banks, each of which has very different objectives and motivations. As of 1992, public and private pensions accounted for 50 percent of the total institutional investment, investment companies accounted for 16 percent, insurance companies accounted for 20 percent, and banks and foundations accounted for the remaining 14 percent (Brancato 1993). These different categories of institutional investors have different federal or state regulations governing their activities and different customer objectives to satisfy (Monks and Minow 1995). As a result, it is very likely that these investors will all have very different investment objectives.

In an important recent study, Kochar and David (1996) were able to identify two different groups of institutional investors: pressure sensitive and pressure resistant. Pressure-sensitive groups were institutional investors such as banks and insurance companies, which, because of their ongoing business relations with the firms in which they invest, are more susceptible to managerial influence. Pressure-sensitive institutional investors were less able to influence firm strategies. Pressure-resistant investors, such as public pension funds, were more concerned about the value of their investments and pressured management to change firm strategies.

In the United States, pension funds are regulated by the U.S. Labor Department's Pension and Welfare Benefits Administration. Their fiduciary duty is defined differently from that of banks or mutual funds (Parker and Givant 1987). In the past, many pension programs were set up as "defined benefit" plans, which promised to pay an employee a fixed payout at some future date. Underfunded pensions must be reported as liabilities on the firm's balance sheet. During a recession, the decline in a firm's pension assets can push the firm toward insolvency. This forced pension fund managers to operate with a short-term objective (Graves and Waddock 1990). In recent years, many firms have moved toward "defined contribution" programs, which promise to annually contribute a certain percentage of the employee's wages to the plan rather than pay out a defined benefit sometime in the future. The defined contribution program greatly reduces the pressure on firms' pension managers to achieve short-term results for their investments.

In the majority of the recent examples of institutional investor activism, it has been the pension fund managers who have initiated actions against management. These actions have included pressuring company management for a variety of reforms, including those affecting governance structure, executive succession, and executive compensation (Monks and Minow 1995). To strengthen their influence over corporate management, these public and private pension funds formed the Council of Institutional Investors in 1985. By 1990 the council included more than sixty pension funds whose assets exceeded $300 billion (Useem 1993).

Bank trust managers have very different classes of beneficiaries with different objectives. Nonetheless, the concerns of most trust managers are dominated by federal income and gift tax issues. Because most trusts are irrevocable, the bank can expect to serve the customer and collect fees regardless of the investment performance. This could explain the historical record of bank trusts, relatively poor performance on equity investments.

Managers of mutual funds have very different motivations since their funds are designed to provide investors with the ability to redeem their shares and receive their money at any time and at the prevailing market price. The performance of mutual fund managers is often evaluated on a quarterly basis, and the resulting turnover among managers is very high (Chaganti, Sherman, and Damanpour 1993). This is not the kind of situation that encourages a long-term relationship between mutual fund managers and the firms in which they invest.

Insurance firms are governed by state laws. They currently can hold only 20 percent of their investments in equities, and they are not allowed to have more than 2 percent of their assets invested in any one firm. Insurance company fund managers have a very strong vested interest in the firms in which they invest. Consequently, they usually hold debt securities in the firms in which they invest and try to develop other commercial business with the firm, such as providing insurance or pension products. Last, unlike mutual funds and pension funds, insurance firms do not have to report how they vote on proxies (Monks and Minow 1995). This allows them to vote with management even though the value of their clients' equity position in the firm may decline in value. Insurance companies and banks are much more likely to support management with regard to antitakeover amendments, even those that hurt the long-term value of the firm (Brickley, Lease, and Smith 1988). Managers of pension funds and mutual funds are more likely to oppose management's actions.

A recent study found that mutual fund investors were only concerned with short-term results (Sherman, Beldona, and Joshi 1996). However, pension funds were found to consistently invest in firms that undertook long-term strategic investments in capital and in research and development expenditures. Hence, not only did they find that institutional owners had different behaviors, but they were found to act in opposite directions.

This would explain why we found that institutional investors did not significantly influence the time taken to initiate a reorientation. However, it is clear that these investors do have the potential to exert a growing influence on the organization. Their ability to affect the firm's actions can best be categorized as "latent" rather than "active" power. Latent power is the ability to constrain certain decision choices. This can be differentiated from active power, which is the power to control the outcome of key decisions regarding the firm's actions. Active power is usually in the hands of the firm's executives and board members.

Institutional owners have the ability to exercise their power in the marketplace by buying or selling a particular firm's securities. A firm's management is well aware that as a result of the sizable holdings institutions usually possess, a sale of these securities could lead to a dramatic drop in the firm's stock price. Furthermore, institutions can influence the firm by directing public pressure campaigns targeted to specific issues. One recent area that institutional investors, led by public pension fund managers, have targeted is reforming the practices of boards of directors.

Lockheed has become a classic example of the role institutional investors can play in the firm's strategic decision process if they choose to exert their latent power. Lockheed became the target of a takeover attempt that was opposed by the firm's management. Harold Simmons and his firm, NL Industries, made an unsuccessful attempt to take over Lockheed in 1989–1991. Simmons wanted to break up the company and sell off the parts since he could obtain more value for the parts than the stock market was currently assigning the whole company.

To win the proxy contest, both Lockheed's management and Simmons had to make concessions in order to win the votes of the company's institutional shareholders. Although Lockheed's management eventually won its proxy battle with investor Harold Simmons, in exchange for their support, institutional shareholders were able to gain an unprecedented permanent voice in running the company.

Lockheed Corporation: The Rising Power of Institutional Investors

In the late 1980s, over 75 percent of Lockheed's sales were dependent on the Pentagon, including major portions of President Reagan's endangered Strategic Defense Initiative. It was clear to all analysts that Lockheed would be increasingly subject to stringent federal-spending limits. During 1986–1988, while the stock market advanced significantly, Lockheed's average annual total return to shareholders amounted to a negative 1.9 percent. Lockheed's backlog was decreasing, and so were earnings. In 1988 the firm had to reduce income by $465 million due to cost overruns on its aircraft programs.

Approximately 45 percent of Lockheed's shares were owned by institutional investors. These shareholders include the pension funds of Bethlehem Steel Corporation and General Electric Company, money managers Sanford C. Bernstein & Company; Loomis Sayles & Company, and public pension funds such as the New York State Teachers' Retirement System and State of Wisconsin Investment Board (Fromson 1990).

To try to bolster the sagging stock price, Lockheed sold off its profitable Dialog Information Services, a database service, for $353 million. The only bright spot was a $5 billion contract the company won to make antisubmarine planes for the navy, but these moves were not enough to impress Wall Street. The stock continued to decline in value. Many investors believed that Lockheed would be the target of a takeover. Daniel Tellep, an engineer who had been with Lockheed for more than thirty years, became the new chief executive officer in January 1989, thus inheriting these problems.

Lockheed's management seemed unaware of how angry its shareholders were with the actions of the board of directors. Institutional investors were especially unhappy with the way Tellep was running Lockheed. He had said that there would be rough times ahead but that in the long term, Lockheed would be an excellent financial performer. Investors were very skeptical as to whether Tellep's strategies were sound. Lockheed's stock price had been trading at only $40 to $55, and its estimated breakup value was $80 (Dobrzynski 1990).

Besides putting up with Lockheed's poor performance, directors had voted for several measures to entrench the current executives. For example, Lockheed reincorporated from California to the more protective state of Delaware and installed a poison pill. As far as shareholders were concerned, the board members had virtually deprived them of all management accountability.

Activist public pension funds submitted shareholder proposals that would remove the company's poison pill, adopt confidential proxy voting, and opt out of the Delaware antitakeover laws, but Tellep and the board had successfully opposed all the shareholders' proposals. Less than a year later investor Harold Simmons began buying stock, accumulating a 0.6 percent stake. On April 3, 1990, Harold C. Simmons announced that he had bought 5.3 percent of Lockheed Corporation and intended to stick around for several years.

Two days later, Lockheed's management unveiled a sweeping restructuring plan. Harold Simmons reduced his stake in the company to 4.2 percent the day after the reorganization was announced, expressing concern over Lockheed's current market performance (Schine 1989).

Simmons requested that he be allowed six seats on the fifteen-person board. Management said no, so Simmons announced his own slate of candidates for the board. Simmons's slate of directors included former senator John Tower and U.S. chief of naval operations Elmo Zumwalt. Simmons also submitted a proposal to rescind the poison pill that Lockheed's management had installed in 1986.

The 45 percent of shares held by the institutional investors would determine the future fate of the organization. Both sides met personally with the institutional investors, offering concessions to win their support. Peg O'Hara, director of the corporate governance service at Investor Responsibility Research Center (an industry association made up of institutional investors), described the situation at Lockheed as a bidding war for institutional investors' support (Parker 1990).

At the stockholder's meeting, Lockheed's Tellep and his management lost on three proposals but won on the crucial issue of whose slate of directors would be elected to the board. Simmons received 36 percent of the vote. The real winners were the institutional investors, who won from Lockheed management an unprecedented promise of three seats on the board, confidential voting on shareholder resolutions, and the elimination of certain antitakeover provisions (Parker 1990).

Tellep realized that in the future he would have to consult the firm's big institutional investors on major strategic decisions. One of the nation's most active institutional investors was the California Public Employees Pension Funds. Dale Hanson, the CEO of CalPERS, recommended that Lockheed set up a special committee consisting of directors and institutional investors to survey a broad sample of shareholders about the qualities they would like to see in a Lockheed director. Tellep accepted the task force's recommendations, and in addition, he asked the institutional investors to develop a list of potential candidates.

As Tellep reported in his *1990 Letter to Shareholders*, "Early in 1990, we pledged to listen and respond to our shareholders' concerns on corporate governance issues. We met these commitments—and then some. We guaranteed confidential voting, revised the shareholder rights plan, and banned greenmail. Most important, after an exhaustive search and consultation with our major institutional shareholders, we elected four excellent new outside directors."

The shareholders vowed to maintain pressure on Tellep. A major institutional owner stated that if things did not improve over the next few years, the next vote might be very different (Parker 1990).

The board did take additional steps to prevent a future takeover. Following the example set in the previous year by Polaroid in its effort to fight a hostile takeover, Lockheed established an employee stock ownership plan, which gave salaried employees about 17 percent of Lockheed's common shares, by far the largest single block of the corporation's stock. The company purchased about 10.5 million shares of newly issued common stock for $500 million to establish the plan, and management stated that this stake could increase substantially over the next fifteen years.

The board claimed that these steps were in the long-term interest of all shareholders and would prevent the company from being taken over by someone who would break it up. The directors had little to lose since out of the twelve outsiders on the board, only three owned meaningful stakes in the company. In this case, the outside board members apparently found it far more comfortable to go along with management rather than challenge it. Clearly, part of the responsibility of the continued poor performance at Lockheed was due to failure on the part of the board to perform its oversight responsibilities.

Reorientation

It was during this period that Tellep embarked on a broad diversification program. Many analysts speculate that one of Tellep's aims was to calm shareholder fears concerning the decline in defense spending. Initially, Tellep pushed deeper into related businesses, such as commercial aircraft maintenance. However, he also began to diversify into unrelated businesses such as nuclear waste cleanup work for the U.S. Energy Department and contracts to dismantle nuclear warheads in the United States and the former Soviet Union. Tellep stated in his *1989 Letter to Shareholders* that "although we will remain primarily a defense contractor, we expect growth in civil space, commercial, and foreign revenues to increase to one third of our sales by the mid-1990s." He made efforts to expand the core businesses of aircraft, missiles, space, and electronics, while tapping potential growth markets such as government services and antisubmarine warfare.

The organization structure was fundamentally altered. Five separate divisions were merged to form a technology services group, which was created to capitalize on the projected growth market in government services such as defense force modernization and maintenance programs. The U.S. Department of Defense had announced that this would be its future area of emphasis as the number of major new defense programs declined.

Tellep sold four of Lockheed's commercial business units, including its profitable information systems group (which included CalComp Group and the CADAM Information Systems Group). Revenues from these sales were to be used to fund a new stock buyback program and the new employee stock program.

Other changes included implementing a new cost-control and contract-pricing system. The workforce was reduced by nearly 6,000 employees and Lockheed Aeronautical Systems Company operations were relocated from Burbank, California, to more efficient facilities. This freed up a prime piece of 225 acres of property in Burbank, which Lockheed sold for about $500 million.

As had been forecasted by industry analysts, the defense industry suffered from reduced demand and major overcapacity. Many of Lockheed's rivals had diversified by converting to civilian production, boosting foreign sales, or selling off their military operations. By 1991, Tellep had put an end to Lockheed's efforts to redefine itself, even though the firm's financial performance was good. Lockheed's efforts to diversify were largely unsuccessful. Its aircraft maintenance unit, for example, stumbled badly as the recession ravaged the airline industry. Its environmental services unit fared poorly because potential customers perceived that cleaning up nuclear waste was not one of Lockheed's strengths, so the subsidiary failed to win any major contracts.

The only major nonmilitary venture that still held promise for Lockheed was its joint venture with Krunichev Enterprise, a Russian rocket company that once launched Soviet spy satellites. This joint venture planned to build sixty-six communications satellites for a global wireless phone system that Motorola intended to have in operation by 1997–1998.

Tellep hoped that this business could grow to generate $1 billion a year by the end of the decade.

Second Reorientation: Success

In 1991 and 1992, Tellep initiated a second reorientation for Lockheed, which reversed the strategic direction of the first reorientation. Tellep announced in 1991 that Lockheed would refocus its efforts on what it knew best: becoming the nation's largest defense contractor (especially in military aircraft). Tellep argued that as more players bailed out of the defense business, there should be enough business to allow a couple of well-focused contractors to prosper. For the short term, Lockheed predicted that regional conflicts would continue to generate a demand for weapons. Tellep felt that Lockheed's core competency in high-tech weapons would give it a clear competitive advantage over the long run and argued that the Pentagon was placing greater emphasis on high-technology systems.

On March 1, 1992, Tellep took a big step toward realizing his goal when Lockheed concluded a $1.5 billion deal to purchase General Dynamic's fighter aircraft division. The acquisition of the General Defense unit, which makes the high-performance F-16 fighter, transformed Lockheed into the largest worldwide military aircraft manufacturer and secured its third-place ranking in the defense business, after McDonnell Douglas and Martin Marietta (Schine 1993). The acquisition increased Lockheed's total sales to about $13 billion and created a $6.5 billion core aeronautical business.

Lockheed would also be able to offer a unique mix of both the leading low-cost fighter (F-16) and the leading advanced-technology fighter (F-22). Moreover, General Dynamics had developed extensive international relationships, which would help Lockheed to sell other products more effectively worldwide. The *1992 Letter to Shareholders* predicted that "as a result, [of the General Dynamics purchase], we anticipate that by the mid-1990s, our business mix will shift from 67 percent to about 55 percent in U.S. defense sales and the balance in international and nondefense activities."

The firm also announced its intention to develop a new corporate culture. Tellep was going to decentralize authority and encourage individual initiative. The firm wanted individuals to initiate new ideas and to make decisions "deliberately and rapidly." For the longer term, instead of emphasizing only cost cutting, Lockheed wanted to manage more wisely.

Mega-Merger

On August 29, 1994, Lockheed merged with Martin Marietta Corporation, which combined the nation's number two and three arms makers.

Martin Marietta had recently acquired General Electric's aerospace division and General Dynamic's space systems unit.

The Pentagon, with the tacit approval of the U.S. Justice Department, had been encouraging the defense contractors to consolidate, as it preferred to rely on a few efficient producers rather than numerous weak ones. With combined annual sales of $23 billion, the new defense firm, Lockheed Martin, would be 50 percent larger than its nearest competitor, McDonnell Douglas. The firm was expected to generate $4 to $5 billion in cash over five years, giving it the resources to make further acquisitions (Borrus 1994). The threat of Lockheed Martin's financial and technology resources was expected to encourage the remaining defense suppliers to seek other combinations in order to be able to compete in this industry.

In April 1996, Lockheed Martin's new CEO, Norman Augustine, announced the purchase of Loral Corporation for $9.1 billion. Lockheed Martin is unquestionably the world's premier defense contractor, amounting to a $27 billion, one-stop weapons store. The firm is now twice the size of its nearest competitor and has been able to obtain an annualized return of 35 percent for the last three years, compared to the Standard & Poors average of 24 percent for the same period.

In all our cases, institutional investors failed to either speed up or slow down the firm's initiation of a reorientation. In a few cases, institutional investors publicly expressed their dissatisfaction with the current management, but we could not identify examples where they appeared to be the initiating force for reorientation.

In the case of Lockheed, the reorientation did not come as a result of pressure from dissatisfied institutional investors but rather as a result of the actions of corporate raiders. The role that institutional investors played was choosing which reorientation would be implemented—the plan of Lockheed's incumbent management or that of Simmons. To win the support of institutional investors, and especially the large public pension funds, Lockheed's management was forced to (at least publicly) become committed to creating shareholder value. Lockheed's management also agreed to regularly meet with large institutional investors to keep them informed and listen to their concerns. In addition, Lockheed reformed the selection process for board members.

Institutional investors do not have the expertise to become active decision-makers in the strategic decision-making process of the firm. It makes more sense for them to seek to reform the board. In the case of Lockheed, the big shareholders drew up a list of potential directors and submitted it to Lockheed's nominating committee—not to the chief executive officer. The result was that the committee chose four new independent, outside directors. It was hoped by shareholders that these board members would take a hard look at Lockheed's strategy and periodically and objectively evaluate the performance of Lockheed's chief executive officer.

THE BOARD OF DIRECTORS AND CORPORATE CHANGE

The board of directors plays two major roles in the corporate governance structure of the firm. The first role, which is determined by law, is the control function. Corporate law requires that the board review and approve management actions to make sure that they are consistent with the interests of shareholders. The advisory board of the National Association of Corporate Directors states that the responsibility of the board of directors is to ensure that the firm establishes long-term strategic plans and objectives and that proper management is in place to achieve them (Vance 1983).

A second function of board, according to the resource dependence theorists (Pfeffer and Salancik 1978), is to provide the firm with access to the resources and expertise it needs to compete successfully. Directors who are members of several different company boards provide the firms' executives with information concerning alternative strategies and organizational practices that are being pursued or considered by related firms and industries. New members need to be appointed to the board as the firm's environment changes (Pfeffer 1986). For example, one study found that firms that needed financial resources had boards consisting of more members who had access to capital and financial markets than resource rich firms (Mizruchi and Stearns 1988).

However, many corporate governance observers contend that too often, the board is only a rubber stamp for the chief executive's decisions and believe that a long-tenured CEO can gain substantial influence over the board's decision-making process (Herman 1981; Mace 1971). The result is that the board often fails to perform its function as an objective external monitor of the actions of the firm's managers (Patton and Baker 1987). Many boards leave strategic planning to the firm's executives and the corporate staff. Several surveys of board practices have found evidence that the chief executive in truth controls the strategic decision-making process (see, for example, Waldo 1985; Harrison 1987; Brown 1982; Andrews 1971).

In more than 75 percent of U.S. corporations, the chief executive officer serves as the chair of the board of directors (Monks and Minow 1996). Since the function of the board is to ensure management accountability, this puts chief executives in the position of overseeing and evaluating themselves. Chief executive officers argue that this is important because it guarantees that each corporation only has one boss. However, it is clear that the separation of these two roles would result in a more objective evaluation of the chief executive's performance. When the CEO is also the board chair, the resulting situation can be likened to students grading their own exams (Monks and Minow 1996).

The chief executive and chairperson of the board can decide when proxy votes are to be requested and how they will be voted. In addition, the chairperson controls the internal operation of the board, nominates all committee chairpersons, and assigns duties to board members (Lorsch 1989). Based on interviews of senior managers of large corporations, the board usually accepts most of management's agenda and shows a readiness to be convinced on the issues that are more controversial (Useem 1993).

Over time, the chief executive gains increasing influence over the members of the board of directors. When a new chief executive is appointed, this executive will most likely inherit a board of directors dominated by individuals loyal to the predecessor. At any given point in time, directors may have allegiances to different individuals, such as the current chief executive, the predecessor, or a dominant stockholder (Fredrickson, Hambrick, and Baumrin 1988). A chief executive who is also the chairperson of the board, however, has the ability to influence the recruitment process and, over time, to eliminate dissenters. Board members who are appointed by the current chief executive will likely feel a need to support him or her for the privilege of being on the board. In addition to compensation, board members are able to develop important business contacts and access to various corporate perks, such as company-owned apartments and jets. The result will be that a long-serving chief executive will end up with a board composed of only directors who are loyal to him.

Recent anecdotal evidence indicates that the rising tide of shareholder power and activism should, in theory, be felt in the boardroom. However, in the majority of cases it appears that boards usually only take action after a firm has experienced prolonged periods of poor performance (Zald 1969; Mintzberg 1983).

In *Fortune* magazine's January 11, 1993 issue, the cover story, titled "The King Is Dead," pronounced the end of the imperial corporate presidency. The story documented situations in which, after years of poor performance, active shareholders pressured board members to take an equally active role in the strategic decision-making process of the firm by replacing the firm's chief executive officer. Companies in which the board has become active include General Motors, Digital Equipment, Goodyear, Tenneco, American Express, and IBM.

Influence of Outside Directors

Many of the observers of the corporate governance process believe that the outside director is the key to establishing effective board oversight of the firm's management. Outside directors are those who are not either currently or formerly managers of the firm. Agency theorists contend that inside directors (the firm's managers), have personal monetary incentives that encourage them to expand the firm's size and diversify its products, even when doing so may fail to result in enhancing shareholder value (Jensen and Murphy 1990). In addition, inside directors will more often participate in developing the firm's current strategies and so will be reluctant to admit the need for change. Insiders will be loyal to their boss, the chief executive officer, who determines their salary and whether they will be promoted.

Outside board members can provide a more objective evaluation of managers' strategic decisions (Baysinger and Hoskisson 1990; Mizruchi 1983). Lacking the history and motives of company insiders, they are more likely to resist actions by management that result in benefiting managers at a cost to shareholder interests (Mizruchi 1983; Monks and Minow 1995). Outside directors play important roles in obtaining scarce resources and in influencing external organizations with which the firm must interact (Pfeffer and Salancik 1978). Jeffrey Pfeffer (1972) observed that firms increased the proportion of outside directors who had associations with financial institutions when they relied more heavily on external financing. Moreover, outsiders bring to the organization different skills and experiences, which can help the firm pursue new opportunities.

A recent well-known example occurred at General Motors (GM), where, after years of poor performance, the outside board members became so concerned that they began to gather their own information concerning GM operations and eventually forced the incumbent chief executive, Roger Stempel, to resign (Ingrassia and White 1994).

We found that outside board members were influential in forcing incumbent management teams to initiate a reorientation more quickly. However, the board usually waited for five to ten years before taking direct action. Board members, whether insiders or outsiders, did not like to intervene in the operation of large firms unless there was a major crisis, and then only after they had repeatedly applied subtle pressure to which the incumbent management had not responded. Often the board waited for the chief executive officer to retire.

The board's influence was also apparent in cases where the firm appointed an outside chief executive, such as AlliedSignal or Tenneco. Obviously, when a chief executive officer from outside the firm takes over, it is a signal to external stakeholders that the board is looking for a change in the strategic direction of the firm. In these cases, the evidence we found indicates that outside board members were the prime movers. These members wanted the board to reverse poor performance by appointing a new chief executive from outside the firm. Thus, they sped up the change process.

Inside board members will actively protect the status quo. In our research, they did not respond quickly to vital changes that had taken place in the firm's environment. As expected, the insiders were more loyal and committed to the firm's existing strategies and policies (Herman 1981; Mizruchi 1983). Therefore, the greater the number of inside directors, the more likely the chief executive officer was to move only slowly to change the firm's strategies.

Out of the nine cases reviewed in detail in this book, four of them (Tenneco, AlliedSignal, Polaroid, and Compaq) had reorientations initiated when an outside chief executive was appointed to replace an incumbent who had been unable to obtain satisfactory results. The first three firms all experienced many years of poor financial performance before the board took action. At Tenneco, the incumbent chief executive officer was only replaced by the board after he had engaged in highly questionable accounting practices. At AlliedSignal, the board did not respond to the poor performance until a financial crisis threatened the survival of the firm. At Polaroid, it was only when the firm experienced an actual profit loss that the chief executive was replaced. The board then named the first outside chief executive officer in Polaroid's history.

Compaq Computers: Successful Board Intervention

The fourth firm, Compaq, took action much more quickly. Of all the companies that we examined, the board of directors at Compaq was the fastest to initiate a reorientation. This board had an outside chairman and was composed mostly of directors who were not employed by Compaq. The personal computer industry was undergoing dramatic changes that required the firm to develop a new strategic direction and new organizational practices or else be over taken by competition. The board responded quickly after it came to realize that the incumbent chief executive, who was also the founder of the firm, did not have the necessary skills. As a result it brought in a new outside chief executive, ousting the founder of Compaq Computer.

Compaq was founded in 1982 by Rod Canion and two other engineers from Texas Instruments. It manufactured and sold the first IBM-compatible portable computer. By 1987, after just five years of operation, the company had passed a billion dollars in sales revenues. Compaq's product strategy was to develop a premium product, priced at the same level as IBM but with the latest technology and features. During the 1980s Canion's team broadened the product line and expanded sales into foreign markets. Instead of building a large sales force, the company selected dealers to which they gave exclusive distributorships. This dealer network proved to be very effective, and by 1990 Compaq had over 3,800 retailers in 152 countries.

Rosen was the venture capitalist who first backed the fledging company. He was a partner in Sevin Rosen Management Company, an investment company that owned about 15 percent of Compaq's shares. By 1987, its ownership share was reduced to less than 1 percent, but Rosen continued to play a very active role as chairman of the board.

The firm ran into difficulty in 1991, when it reported the first-ever quarterly loss. Economic recession, domestic price wars, and slowing overseas sales all played a part in causing Compaq's revenues and profits to decline faster than those of its competitors. Large customers were no longer willing to pay premiums of 20 to 30 percent for Compaq machines when they could get clones that were almost as good. Compaq's stock price dropped by 60 percent.

Canion planned a massive internal reorganization to put the company back to the leading position, but the board of directors, still chaired by Rosen, came to the decision that Compaq's problems and the current market required someone with more marketing experience. Canion was forced to resign. He was replaced by Eckhard Pfeiffer, an engineer and former marketing head from Texas Instruments who had joined Compaq in 1983 and later became the chief of its hugely successful international operations. Pfeiffer immediately initiated a reorientation (beginning in 1992).

Reorientation

Nine hours after Pfeiffer took over control as the chief executive officer, he convened a task force to start planning for the company's new line of personal computers. His new strategy was to be the low-cost and high-volume industry leader. Pfeiffer was going to meet the low-cost clones head-on. He told his employees he would not accept incremental change. Companies like Dell Computer had begun to sell direct to customers by mail and phone, offering solid support and service programs as well as unbelievably low prices.

Compaq announced that it would move away from its exclusive dealer network and offer products for sale through discounters, direct mail, and mass merchandisers. The strategic emphasis for the firm shifted from technology and innovation to marketing.

The firm announced that it would be reorganized into two divisions, low-cost personal computers and more sophisticated computer systems. To implement this strategy, Pfeiffer implemented strict cost controls. The method of designing and building computers was completely reengineered. The company introduced the concept of employee empowerment and created high-performance work teams. Decision making was pushed to lower levels to facilitate faster product development cycles.

Aftermath: Startling Success

In 1994, Compaq Computers exceeded the $10 billion sales level and the company achieved its 1992 objective of becoming the number one producer of personal computers in the world—larger than either Apple or IBM. Compaq's performance was stunning: in a year of price wars and continuing industry consolidation, its net income increased 88 percent and sales by 51 percent.

The firm continued to restructure to meet its objective of becoming the world's leading low-cost provider. Productivity and quality continued to be improved, and the new, totally redesigned desktops now took half the time to be built (10.5 minutes in 1994 versus 21.0 minutes in 1992). Compaq introduced forty new products, such as microprocessors, computer memory boards, and disk drives.

In 1995, in a major effort to expand its business, Compaq introduced more than 100 new and redesigned models. Pfeiffer then announced a new round of price cuts, ranging from 8 to 23 percent. Sales reached $14.8 billion, and net income hit $1 billion, which made Compaq the third most profitable company in the United States. The board of directors almost doubled Pfeiffer's annual compensation, from $2.50 to $5.05 million.

In 1996, the company was still growing at twice the rate of the industry, with sales exceeding $18 billion. However, profits remained unchanged from the previous year. Hewlett-Packard, IBM, and others were going after Compaq's profitable server business, which had accounted for more than 50 percent of the firm's profits. The server is a computer or device on a network that manages network resources. The most well-known types include file, print, and network servers. The print server manages one or more printers, and a network server manages network traffic.

Pfeiffer, in his *1996 Letter to Shareholders*, established Compaq's new corporate goal: "To be one of three global computer companies by the year 2000." In a key strategic change, Pfeiffer wanted Compaq to set the pace in new digital TV and home personal computers, challenging the industry leaders, IBM and Hewlett-Packard.

To meet his aggressive goal of 20 to 25 percent growth per year, Pfeiffer created nine new divisions. These divisions would concentrate on new growth areas such as Internet products and engineering workstations. Pfeiffer expressed the desire to maintain the nimbleness of the small company and yet have the service and product offerings of a computer giant. He argued that this was the key turning point in Compaq's history. His goal was to reach $40 billion in revenues in the year 2000.

In 1997, analysts expected Compaq to generate $22 billion in sales, with profits reaching $1.7 billion. The company was expanding into networking though its acquisitions of networking products makers Net-worth (hubs and switches) and Thomas-Conrad (sellers of interface cards and hubs).

Compaq was unique in our study. In all the other cases we examined, the chief executive officer was also the chairperson of the board. The result was that the board was run by the person it was to evaluate. Compaq was the only case where the board acted very quickly in ousting the incumbent chief executive officer and appointing a new CEO. Compaq's board was composed primarily of outside directors and was directed by a chairperson who was also an outsider. For corporate governance observers and business practitioners, Compaq Computer provides a prescription of how the board of directors should be constituted.

5

Toward a More Responsive Corporate Governance System

American enterprise must fundamentally rethink the way in which it conducts business. Market stability is threatened by government deregulation, increased global competition, short product life cycles, new technologies, the frequent entry of unexpected outsiders and repositioning by incumbents, scientific breakthroughs, and changes in consumer lifestyles.

Today competition is based on time. "Time is a fundamental business performance variable" (Stalk and Hout 1990, 39). Consequently, speed has become a critical competitive advantage. Futurists such as Alvin Toffler (1990) predicted that in the future, only the "fast" firms will succeed. In an interview with *Business Week* in 1993, Bill Gates, chief executive officer of Microsoft, said that the success of a firm depends, not on how large the company is, but rather on its ability to aggressively move to each successive competitive advantage.

The result is few industry leaders who started the 1980s entered the 1990s with their executive team still intact. American Telephone and Telegraph (AT&T), Xerox, General Motors, Sears, Digital Equipment, and IBM are just a few examples of firms whose leadership positions have been destroyed. Investors in these firms have seen billions of dollars in shareholder value lost because the executive teams often failed to respond quickly to these changes.

The 1980s and the 1990s represent a pivotal period in which American enterprises permanently changed their definition of responsiveness. Past research found that major change has taken decades to complete

(Child and Smith 1987; Pettigrew 1985), but this is no longer true. We found that reorientations, even in relatively large organizations, are not rare. They occur routinely and in shorter periods of time. In our sample of 100 corporations, thirty (30 percent) had experienced a reorientation during the period 1985–1992. In addition, out of these thirty firms, ten (30 percent) had experienced an additional reorientation in the period 1992–1996.

Reorientation used to be thought of as an unusual occurrence that large firms implemented only a few times over their entire history and only when they faced a crisis situation. Today, however, reorientations are being implemented quickly to exploit new opportunities or respond to new threats. Shareholders and board members are demanding that their firm's management respond in as timely a manner as possible to competitive developments.

As a matter of fact, all 100 firms in our sample—even those that had not implemented a reorientation—were routinely changing one of their major corporate elements approximately every two years, be it corporate strategy, control systems, or corporate structure. These changes were being made regardless of the firms' previous performance levels.

As a result, firms must build capabilities for learning and self-renewal. We expect to find that successful firms will be those that are able to develop the capabilities to change in "real time." This will require an improved corporate governance system, whose participants must be quicker to intervene if the incumbent management fails to respond to changes in its competitive environment.

In this chapter, we first review the similarities in the content that reorientations have taken. We also discuss recent trends that have occurred, which lead us to conclude that a more balanced and responsive corporate governance system is being put in place in many of the largest corporations across America.

CONTENT OF REORIENTATION

We found that many of the changes being made to the firm's strategies, structure, and control systems were following similar patterns. These patterns are discussed below.

Strategy

During the 1960s and 1970s, many large corporations pursued a corporate strategy of diversification into unrelated products and markets. At the time it was thought that a good professional manager had the necessary skills to run any business, regardless of the industry. During this time, conglomerates such as Textron, Gulf & Western, and ITT were growing rapidly and very profitably.

By the 1980s there was growing skepticism among investors concerning the ability of managers of unrelated conglomerates to create shareholder value. Corporate raiders such as Carl Icahn and T. Boone Pickens showed that they could realize substantial profits by taking over diverse businesses and selling off unrelated units. To prevent hostile takeovers of their firms, many management teams renounced the strategy of product market diversification and refocused their investment on their core businesses.

General Mills's management found, in their internal study, that the more diversified a firm had become, the more average was its financial performance. In the examples that we reviewed, General Mills was the first to refocus (1984–1985), which it did by spinning off its toy and fashion clothing businesses to shareholders and concentrating on food and restaurants.

Several of the firms discussed in this book, such as Allied, Polaroid, Lockheed, and Baxter, went in the opposite direction of this trend. Hennessey, at Allied, took a chemical company and turned it into a highly diversified conglomerate. At Polaroid, Booth tried to diversify from instant photography to electronic imaging. Both strategies proved unsuccessful and were later reversed. In the cases of Lockheed and Baxter, both were facing environments that had suddenly become very hostile. As a result of significant government cutbacks, Lockheed, as well as other defense firms, tried to enter into new nondefense-related industries. Baxter responded to increased pressure in the health care industry to contain costs. It diversified into new product lines in an attempt to become "a one-stop shop" for its hospital customers. For both companies the diversification efforts proved unsuccessful and had to be reversed.

Organization Structures and Control Systems

The value of the reorientation concept is that it recognizes that it is insufficient for firms to simply change their corporate strategy. A new context must be created that consistently encourages employees to behave and think in the desired direction. All elements of the organization—its employees, structure, corporate culture, and control systems—must support each other and be congruent with the firm's overall strategic orientation.

In today's new competitive environment, firms have been developing new approaches to organizing. One major trend that we identified—and that continues today—is that all firms are trimming corporate staff and middle management positions and pushing the responsibility for decision making to lower levels of the organization. Top management is increasingly granting operating units greater autonomy, with unit managers given discretion over all the resources their unit requires to do its work. This increases the speed with which the firm can react to competitive change. Organizations no longer have the time for lengthy communication and debate. Bossidy at Allied is a prime example, with a philosophy of "let[ting] action happen where it can happen the quickest and most effectively" (*1996 Letter to Shareholders*). This meant eliminating layers of management, establishing cross-functional teams, and delegating decision making for speed and creativity. This demand for high-performance targets and unrelenting focus on customer satisfaction has begun to replace the more comfortable routines of the 1960s and 1970s.

We also found that two new control systems were being implemented in many of the companies: total quality management systems and new executive and management compensation systems that focus attention more clearly on improving shareholder value. These efforts to change the corporate-wide control systems are targeted at instilling a new employee orientation toward customer satisfaction in terms of speed, quality, service, and cost.

Total quality management programs have been installed in many of the Fortune 500 companies. In the cases we reviewed, Bossidy at Allied-Signal, Walsh at Tenneco, and Schacht at Cummins Engine all implemented corporate-wide total quality management programs. At AlliedSignal, within just two years, all 90,000 employees had completed an initial two-day training program. Employees were encouraged to identify and eliminate unnecessary work and to find ways to improve customer service. At Cummins, Schacht endorsed many of the Japanese manufacturing techniques, including a continuous quality improvement program. He invested heavily in employee training, flexible manufacturing, and just-in-time inventory systems.

When a firm delegates decision making to lower levels of the organization, it eliminates supervisory positions. That means eliminating a level of control. As a replacement to this control system, corporations have come to rely more heavily on new compensation systems to align the interests of management with shareholders. Everyone is required to justify their decisions on the basis of the anticipated impact they will have on shareholder value. Polaroid and Phillips are examples of firms that have begun to use economic value added as their decision criteria. Companies like to Polaroid are tying their performance and incentive systems to improvements in shareholder value. The result is that management interests have become more closely aligned with the interests of shareholders.

Another incentive system that many firms were implementing were employee stock ownership programs (ESOPs). Three of the firms in our sample, Polaroid, Phillips, and Lockheed, established ESOPs to prevent current or future takeover attempts. These programs transfer large portions of stock ownership from outside shareholders to the firm's employees. The purpose of ESOPs is to motivate employees (now shareholders themselves) and managers to think and make decisions as though their own money were at stake. Employees who are stockholders are expected to be more productive and less resistant to implementing major change due to expectations that the stock they own will improve in value. It is possible that in a relatively short period of time, ESOPs can acquire a substantial amount of stock. In the case of Lockheed, the ESOP was specifically designed to make the employees the majority stockholder and avert takeover attempts.

TRIGGERS OF REORIENTATION

There are five key elements that influence the time taken to initiate a reorientation.

Performance

As we expected, the firm's prior financial performance establishes an environment in which executives, board members, and major shareholders are motivated to initiate massive change in organizational strategies and practices. The magnitude and nature of a firm's financial problems are used by managers to signal how quickly this must be accomplished.

Executives, board members, and shareholders all appear to have different levels of expectations for firm performance. In this research, performance was poor for at least three years or more before most executives considered it necessary to initiate a reorientation. As performance declined, the sense of urgency increased and change got under way more quickly. We also found that a comprehensive measure of performance, Altman's Z, was a much more accurate way to predict when the firm's executives would have this sense of urgency. If Altman's Z was declining for several years, then the firm was perceived to be facing a crisis and in need of massive change to be implemented immediately.

Importance of the CEO

The fastest and most successful reorientations were those that were initiated by an incumbent, proactive chief executive officer. These executives usually had been in office for several years and were able to establish a firm power base. They had also developed an in-depth understanding of their industry and their company. Therefore, they had the ability to initiate a reorientation much more quickly and effectively than a new chief executive who is brought in from outside the firm. In the example of Cummins Engine, the incumbent chief executive officer was able to initiate a reorientation proactively. At Cummins Engine, Schacht clearly emerged as an outstanding leader. He had the vision and commitment to set and meet tough performance standards that took Cummins years to achieve. He never lost sight of his vision; rather, he stayed his course and accomplished the near-impossible task of preventing the Japanese from gaining any foothold in the U.S. market.

The importance of personal leadership in initiating reorientation cannot be overstated. In most of the cases that we examined the chief executive officer stepped forward, took the initiative, and carried through. The leader can affect the energy that goes into the change process—how it is generated and sustained—which, in many cases, determines the outcome of the reorientation process.

In the few cases where a firm possessed a charismatic, visionary chief executive, he or she stood out very clearly from the others. The people we found in this category exhibited courage, foresight, energy, and an unwavering conviction that allowed them to implement a reorientation quickly, often before the firm's performance had begun to decline.

At AlliedSignal and Compaq Computer, outside chief executives were brought in to initiate a reorientation. However, in both cases, after they had been in their respective positions for over five years, the CEOs both initiated a second reorientation even though both firms were still exhibiting superior financial performance. These men—Pfeiffer at Compaq and Bossidy at AlliedSignal—are outstanding executives. If you read their speeches and examine their actions, their drive and commitment to excellence and to their customers distinguish them from other CEOs.

Corporate Raiders

Of the Fortune 500 manufacturers listed in 1980, 143 were the target of at least one takeover attempt by 1990 (Useem 1993). These outside investors were convinced that many large U.S. corporations were being managed by entrenched executives who were not achieving satisfactory returns for their shareholders. They saw an opportunity to take over these firms, implement major change, and realize substantial returns on their investments. The message sent by these corporate raiders was clear: management had to at least appear to be taking steps to satisfy the existing shareholders.

In our sample, corporate raiders often tried to take control of firms that had experienced many years of poor performance and whose long-tenured executives had failed to implement major changes to the firm's practices. The raiders saw an opportunity to pursue a different strategy and obtain substantial returns.

Corporate raiders certainly hastened the move toward reorientation, but they rarely added value to this process. The most unsuccessful reorientations occurred in firms that made big changes in an attempt to fight off takeover attempts. Their subsequent performance continued to be poor, and in most cases, the board was forced to appoint a new chief executive officer, who invariably reversed the strategic direction. One example was Polaroid, which implemented a reorientation to fight off a takeover attempt by Shamrock Holdings. Polaroid decided to diversify, becoming involved in products that were associated with electronic imaging. After years of very poor performance, however, a newly appointed outside chief executive officer reversed the strategic direction and Polaroid once again became focused on only the instant photography industry. The CEO also made dramatic improvements in the firm's practices that allowed the original strategy to again become effective. Interestingly, this was exactly the strategy that the corporate raider Shamrock Holdings would have implemented had its takeover bid been accepted.

Even when the result of a takeover attempt is a better-run company, it can come at a very high cost. In many cases, the steps incumbent management took to fight off the corporate raiders caused shareholder value to decline dramatically. Perhaps the most devastating example occurred at Phillips Petroleum, which had to fight off a pair of back-to-back takeover attempts. The firm incurred so much debt by paying greenmail and by building future takeover defenses that it greatly increased the risk of going bankrupt. Shareholder value was thus sacrificed for management independence.

Institutional Investors

The most dramatic change in corporate ownership in the past fifty years has been the shift of stock ownership in the last decade and a half to institutional owners. These institutional owners have the ability to exercise power in the marketplace by buying or selling a particular firm's securities. A sale of these large holdings could lead to a dramatic drop in the firm's stock price. Furthermore, institutions can influence the firm by directing public pressure campaigns targeted to specific issues. It is clear that institutional investors often control enough of a firm's outstanding stock to force its management to accept a new strategic direction.

We found that up until the early 1990s, however, institutional investors had not yet used their power to trigger major reorientations. Since these shareholders generally do not have the time or access to all the information needed to properly evaluate a firm's strategies and practices, they take longer to conclude that the current management is not responding properly to environmental changes. It would be rare for them to have the expertise and in-depth industry knowledge to actually direct firm strategies.

The institutional investors' influence can nonetheless be considerable, as the Lockheed case demonstrates. Although institutional investors had been expressing their dissatisfaction with the firm's management, it was a corporate raider that forced the firm to initiate a reorientation. Before the institutional investors agreed to vote in support of the incumbent management, they required it to reform the board of directors to make it more responsive to the interests of shareholders.

Only recently has there been evidence to suggest that unhappy institutional investors are becoming effective at targeting corporate executives who fail to quickly address performance. For example, the October 3, 1996 issue of the *Wall Street Journal* reported that institutional investors were pressuring Viacom to sell off a relatively recent acquisition, Blockbuster Video (purchased in 1994 for $8 billion). Capital Resource Group, which owns a 7.8 percent stake in Viacom, was urging the company's management to focus on movies and cable TV business and to spin off the lower-margin, slower-growth video rental business. Viacom has since announced that it will begin listing the stock of Blockbuster separately from that of Viacom.

In addition, a September 30, 1996 *Wall Street Journal* article reported that institutional owners were pressuring Pepsico to sell off its restaurant business. A fund manager told Pepsico's management that none of the institutional investors understand how the restaurant business fit with the rest of the firm's businesses and that Pepsico was not managing the business well. At the time, Roger Enrico, Pepsico's chief executive officer, said that the firm had no intention of selling off the division, but within nine months, Pepsico announced plans to spin off the division to shareholders.

Board of Directors

According to law, a corporate board of directors is elected by the shareholders to select managers and to approve strategies intended to optimize the return to shareholders. We found that the board of directors generally failed to act consistently with the interests of shareholders. All too often, it accepted management's position and failed to respond quickly to the firm's poor performance.

Interestingly, in the majority of cases where the board finally responded by appointing a new chief executive officer, the firm achieved outstanding financial performance. The successful examples we reviewed included Bossidy at AlliedSignal, Pfeiffer at Compaq Computers, Walsh at Tenneco, and DiCamillo at Polaroid.

Therefore, even though the board of directors was generally not effective in requiring a firm's management to initiate a reorientation in a timely manner, once they did act, the results, in terms of the firm's subsequent performance, were excellent. Corporate reformers and shareholders would do well to focus their attention on making the board of directors more objective and timely in their actions; in other words, making it do what it was designed to do.

RECENT TRENDS IN THE CORPORATE GOVERNANCE SYSTEM

To compete successfully into the twenty-first century, firms must develop the capacity to change quickly and effectively. This means that the corporate governance process will have to become more responsive to shareholders' interests. The solution lies, most importantly, with the firm's executive team and a rejuvenated board of directors. Fortunately, we see recent evidence to indicate that in general, firm's executives and boards of directors are becoming more responsive, largely as a result of the efforts of institutional investors who use their influence to reform board practices.

The largest pension funds got together in 1985 and formed the Council of Institutional Investors, an association of public and private pension funds. The purpose of the group is to promote reform in the corporate governance process to increase firm responsiveness to shareholders. By 1990, the council had sixty members whose combined assets exceeded $300 billion. In recent years the council has recommended several approaches that its members can take to make boards more responsive to their interests.

In 1994, the National Association of Corporate Directors (NACD) published a report on how directors and boards should be evaluated. The report was prepared by a blue ribbon panel of directors, shareholders, and academics. It urged boards to develop a system for evaluating directors and compensation approaches as well as a separate evaluation of the roles of the chief executive officer and chair of the board, even if the position is held by the same person.

Three key areas likely to undergo the most reform are the chairperson's role, the director's experience and independence, and the director's compensation. The top reform on many investors' lists is the separation of the role of the chief executive officer from that of chair of the board. If these two positions are combined, the board, which is responsible for *supervising* management will actually be *led* by management. This obviously hampers the board's ability to be objective and independent.

Only 20 percent of U.S. corporations have separated these two positions (Bacon 1990). In our research, only one firm, Compaq Computer, did so. In this case, the outcome underscored the value of this reform, as the board responded quickly and effectively.

The second reform for which investors are calling is an increase in the number of directors who are not employed by the firm or have any actual or potential financial dealing with it. It is not enough that the directors be employed outside the firm—they also must be independent of the chief executive officer. Additionally, directors must have the knowledge and experience to be able to challenge the firm's management.

In addition, directors must have access to whatever information they need to make an objective evaluation of the firm's executives. They cannot rely on the chief executive as the sole source for the information on which they base the executive's performance evaluation. One approach that has been used is the appointment of a "lead" director. This person could be a retired chief executive officer who is knowledgeable and highly respected by both the board and management. He or she would act as a "shadow" chief executive officer, requesting information independently from the firm's executives.

An example of this approach occurred informally in 1992 at General Motors. John Smale, the former chief executive officer of Procter & Gamble, played the role of the lead outside director. After many years of continued poor performance, Smale began to seek his own information as to what was happening inside of the firm. He refused to accept only the information that was being provided in the four-hour board meetings. This helped him convince the rest of the outside board members that Roger Stempel, General Motor's chief executive officer at the time, should not continue as chair of the board. Smale took over as chair, and several months later, the board replaced Roger Stempel as chief executive officer.

Last, to get directors to think like the owners they are supposed to represent, reforms should include a contingent compensation system. Directors should receive a larger portion of their compensation based on stock options rather than a flat fee. Lockheed has started paying directors at least partly in stock. This is similar to the approach that is advocated to get management to align its interests more closely with those of the shareholders.

CONCLUSION

Jack Welch, the chief executive officer of General Electric, said of the decade of the 1990s: "It's going to be brutal. When I said a while back that the 1980s were going to be the white-knuckled decade and the 1990s would be even tougher, I may have understated how hard it's going to be" (D'Aveni 1994, 5). In today's globally competitive environment, massive organizational change is a requirement for firms to be able to survive. The ability of firms to formulate and implement the change process more effectively and ahead of competitors has become the overriding competitive advantage.

Robert Crandall, chief executive officer of American Airlines, told *Business Week* in 1992: "This business is intensely, vigorously, bitterly, savagely competitive. American's success depends on moving quickly from one advantage to the next" (Zellner and Rothman 1992, 50). To do so, firms will have to make the most of their human resources. Although change may start as a result of pressure from shareholders, it is the inside decision makers—the incumbent chief executive officer and board of directors—who hold the real power to make massive change successfully and on a timely basis.

Appendix A

Overview of the Changes That Occurred in American Manufacturing Firms

The study of 100 diversified manufacturing firms over a seven-year period (1985–1991) points to the following trends:

- As shown in Table A.1, 30 percent of the firms completed a reorientation (changed their strategy, structure, and systems within a time frame of two years), whereas the remaining 70 percent did not.

- In the case of the firms that reoriented, it took them an average of 4.07 years before they responded to deteriorating performance. The results indicate that reorientations, even in relatively large organizations, are not rare and indeed appear to occur routinely.

- All firms examined in this book, even those that did not reorient, took an average of seven years to change all three dimensions (structure, control systems, and strategy).

- There is a high correlation between the stock ownership of inside owners, 5 percent blockholders, and institutional owners (see Table A.8).

- As Table A.1 shows, mean tenures of the chief executive officer (CEO) and top management team (TMT) are long. Not unrelated to the above, the percentage of top management team members appointed by the CEO is almost 59 percent and the percentage of board members is 47 percent.

- The Cox proportional hazard method models hazard rates (the likelihood that an event will take place). Therefore, a negative coefficient obtained using the Cox method is interpreted in the following manner. As the prior performance decreases, the hazard (likelihood) that a firm will initiate a reorientation will increase. That is, as prior performance declines, the time it takes a firm to initiate a reorientation will decrease. The results presented in Table A.2 show that a deterioration in a firm's financial condition, as indicated by Altman's Z, tends to hasten the initiation of a reorientation. However, as shown in Table A.3, change in return on assets (ROA) and time taken to initiate reorientation are positively related. The differences in the findings suggest that top management of the multidivisional firms like the ones represented in the study do not respond quickly to changes in a single measure of performance (e.g., ROA) but do respond to changes in composite indicators (as measured by Altman's Z).

- In firms with relatively high prior performance, the presence of 5 percent blockholders and time taken to initiate reorientation are negatively related (Tables A.4 and A.5). That is, 5 percent blockholders tend to slow managements' initiation of a reorientation when performance is superior. We did not find a significant association in the firms with relatively low prior performance.

- However, there is a significant difference between the levels of 5 percent blockholders in firms that did reorient versus those that did not. In firms in which reorientation occurred, only about 10 percent of the stock was held by big blockholders. This compares to 18.5 percent of the stock being held by the blockholders in firms in which reorientation did not occur. This suggests that blockholders sell their stock before firms initiate reorientations.

- As shown in Tables A.6 and A.7, in firms that are experiencing relatively low performance, the presence of outside directors and CEOs hired from outside the organization tended to shorten the time the firm took to initiate a reorientation.

Table A.1

Firms That Have Experienced Reorientation versus Firms That Did Not: A Comparison

	Firms That Experienced Reorientation		Firms That Did Not Experience Reorientation	
Initial Conditions (As of 1985)	Mean	Standard Deviation	Mean	Standard Deviation
5% Blockholder Ownership	10.42	11.05	18.54	19.15
% Inside Ownership	4.98	8.72	6.43	10.35
% Institutional Ownership	42.62	18.47	40.87	16.79
CEO Outside Successor	0.25	0.44	0.14	0.35
Board Member's Tenure	8.98	3.87	3.57	3.55
CEO Tenure in Position	7.96	7.16	7.63	6.29
CEO Tenure with Firm	23.14	13.05	24.27	11.01
TMT Tenure	16.69	8.56	17.42	5.89
% of Board Members Appointed by CEO	46.81	31.06	45.88	27.69
% of TMT Members Appointed by CEO	64.90	28.63	61.13	25.95
Prior Performance Average in Altman's Z (1983-1985)	3.86	1.93	3.85	2.16
Prior Performance, Change in Altman's Z (1983-1985)	-0.76	1.73	-0.02	0.80
Prior Performance, Average ROA (1983-1985)	0.79	0.45	1.01	0.80
Prior Performance, Change in ROA (1983-1985)	1.53	5.82	-0.35	4.92
Number of Firms	29		71	

Table A.2
Relationship of Altman's Z to the Time It Takes the Firm to Initiate a Reorientation (Cox Proportional Hazard Model with Dependent)

Independent Variables			Change in Altman's Z as the Performance Measure	
			Maximum Likelihood Estimate	Standard Error
1983 - 1985 Firm Performance			-0.41****	0.15
Log Likelihood	With Covariates	185.20		
	Without Covariates	192.95		
	df	98		
	p	0.005		

Note: The only variable entered into model was the prior performance measure.
*$p < 0.10$; **$p < 0.05$; ***$p < 0.01$; ****$p < 0.001$

Table A.3
Relationship of Change in ROA to the Time It Takes the Firm to Initiate a Reorientation (Cox Proportional Hazard Model with Dependent Variable: Time)

		Change in ROA as the Performance Measure	
Independent Variables		Maximum Likelihood Estimate	Standard Error
1983-1985 Firm Performance		0.09**	0.05
Log Likelihood	With Covariates	195.49	
	Without Covariates	199.36	
	df	99	
	p	0.05	

Note: The only variable entered into the model was the prior performance measure.
$* p < 0.10; ** p < 0.05; *** p < 0.01; **** p < 0.001$

Table A.4
High Performers—Change in Altman's Z and the Relationship of Governance Variables to the Time Taken to Initiate Reorientation (Cox Proportional Hazard Model Analysis of Firms with High Prior Performance Only and Dependent Variable: Time)

Independent Variables		Change in Altman's Z as the Performance Measure	
		Maximum Likelihood Estimate	Standard Error
5 % Blockholders		-0.05*	0.03
Log Likelihood	With Covariates	57.67	
	Without Covariates	62.75	
	df	45	
	p	0.03	

Note: Other covariates entered into this model were: 5% blockholders, % of outside board members, origin of CEO, TMT tenure, and control variables (firm size and environmental volatility).
*$p < 0.10$; ** $p < 0.05$; *** $p < 0.01$; **** $p < 0.001$*

Table A.5
High Performers—Change in ROA and the Relationship of Governance Variables to the Time Taken to Initiate Reorientation (Cox Proportional Hazard Model Analysis of Firms with Dependent Variable: Time)

		Change in ROA as the Performance Measure	
Independent Variables		Maximum Likelihood Estimate	Standard Error
5% Block Holders		-0.06**	0.03
TMT Tenure		-0.10**	0.05
Log Likelihood	With Covariates	79.46	
	Without Covariates	90.34	
	df	46	
	p	0.004	

Note: Other covariates entered into this model were 5% blockholders, % of outside board members, origin of CEO, TMT tenure and control variables (firm size and environmental volatility).
*$p < 0.10$; ** $p < 0.05$; *** $p < 0.01$; **** $p < 0.001$

Table A.6

Low Performers—Change in Altman's Z and the Relationship of Governance Variables to the Time Taken to Initiate Reorientation (Cox Proportional Hazard Model with Dependent Variable: Time)

Independent Variables			Change in Altman's Z as the Performance Measure	
			Maximum Likelihood Estimate	Standard Error
Outside Board of Directors			0.05*	0.03
Outside CEO Successor			1.10*	0.59
Log Likelihood	With Covariates	73.95		
	Without Covariates	78.64		
	df	47		
	p	0.03		

Note: Variables entered into this model were 5% blockholders, % of outside board members, origin of CEO, TMT tenure, and control variables (firm size and environmental volatility).
*p < 0.10; **p < 0.05; ***p < 0.01; ****p < 0.001*

Table A.7
Low Performers—Change in ROA and the Relationship of
Governance Variables to the Time Taken to Initiate Reorientation
(Cox Proportional Hazard Model with Dependent Variable: Time)

Independent Variables			Change in ROA as the Performance Measure	
			Maximum Likelihood Estimate	Standard Error
Outside Board of Directors			0.06*	0.03
Log Likelihood	With Covariates	68.90		
	Without Covariates	73.04		
	df	46		
	p	0.04		

Note: Other covariates entered into this model were 5% blockholders, % of outside board members, origin of CEO, TMT tenure and control variables (firm size and environmental volatility).
*p < 0.10; **p < 0.05; ***p < 0.01; ****p < 0.001*

103

Table A.8
Means, Standard Deviations, and Pearson Correlations:

Governance Conditions as of 1985	Mean	SD	1	2	3	4	5	6	7	8	9	10
1. 5% Block Holders	16.21	17.5										
2. Institutional Investors (%)	41.37	17.2	0.24*									
3. CEO Origin	0.17	0.38	0.02	-0.15								
4. Board Members Tenure	9.40	6.64	0.34***	-0.06	-0.01							
5. CEO Tenure	23.95	11.5	-0.04	0.09	-0.49***	0.20*						
6. TMT Tenure	17.22	6.70	-0.10	0.23*	-0.40***	0.21*	0.68***					
7. Origin of Board members	59.90	15.9	-0.26***	0.12	0.03	-0.42***	-0.18	-0.05				
8. % Insider Ownership	6.02	9.78	0.65***	-0.26**	0.02	0.28**	0.02	0.12	-0.38***			
9. CEO Tenure in Position	7.72	6.52	0.10	-0.20*	0.28**	0.24*	0.16	-0.10	-0.21*	0.31**		
10. % of Board of Members Appointed by CEO	46.14	28.5	0.07	-0.23*	0.33***	-0.22*	-0.02	-0.28**	-0.10	0.18	0.63***	
11. % of TMT Appointed by CEO	62.21	26.6	0.06	-0.14	0.17	-0.01	0.02	-0.18	-0.21*	0.14	0.63***	0.48***

$*p < 0.05$; $**p < 0.01$; $***p < 0.001$

Appendix B

Methodology

RESEARCH DESIGN

The study reported in this book was intended to investigate the influence that different participants in the governance system have on the time it takes a firm to initiate a reorientation. This question is process oriented, as it examines the relative effects of prior firm performance and changes in the governance structure on subsequent organizational behavior. This research attempts to establish a temporal sequence of the events before a reorientation occurs; therefore, a longitudinal design was used. A major advantage of longitudinal research is that temporal precedence can be established, at least within the constraints of the study's data.

The study examined major corporations from 1983 to 1985 to establish prior firm financial performance. The initial governance characteristics were measured in 1985. All other variables were examined over the time period of 1985 to 1991. In order to investigate whether the timeliness of the initiation of reorientation affected subsequent performance, we further examined a selected group of firms for the period of 1992 to 1996.

Data Collection

Firm financial performance and industry sales data were taken from the Standard & Poor's Compustat Industrial Data Base. The information concerning the percent of outstanding stock owned by institutional investors was taken from *Standard & Poor's Stock Guide*. Firm proxy statements and annual reports provided the source for all other variables: governance changes, time of reorientation, and control variables. Since proxy materials seek to solicit stockholder approval for the selection of directors and officers, these documents provide extensive information about the firm's top managers and directors and any major changes in firm operating practices (Lant, Milliken, and Batra 1992). Industry journals and general business press articles verified that the reorientation had occurred. Virany, Tushman, and Romanelli found that reorientations were "sufficiently encompassing to stand out yearly in both public and private records from the more routine organization changes" (1992, 81).

Sample Selection

This sample consists of forty-seven firms from industries that are categorized as having low environmental volatility and fifty-three firms from industries that are categorized as having high volatility. Previous research found that environment can be an important variable in explaining corporate change. The sample used in this research was chosen to accentuate the differences between high- and low-volatility environments.

The first step in the selection of the sample was to identify two groups of industries, at the four-digit standard industrial code (SIC) level, that represented significant differences in environmental volatility.

Data was collected from the U.S. Bureau of Census on the dollar value of product shipped by all producers in each selected SIC code for the years 1983–1991. The coefficient of variation in sales was calculated for over seventy-five of the four-digit SIC codes. The coefficient of variation is calculated as the standard deviation divided by the mean. The sample included only SIC codes that had at least seven firms listed in the Compustat Industrial Database for all the years under study. If the coefficient was high, the industry was considered to have a volatile environment. This approach was used by Lant, Milliken, and Batra (1992).

The next step was to arrange the SIC codes in order, from the lowest value coefficient of variation to the highest. Starting with the lowest value, industries were selected until forty-seven firms were identified as being in more stable industries (the sample was to consist of forty-seven firms that were in stable environments and fifty-three in turbulent environments). Only manufacturers listed on the New York Stock Exchange were selected to assure the availability of the needed data and because one of the purposes of this study was to examine large U.S. corporations.

The final sample consists of forty-seven firms from thirteen industries that have relatively stable environments. The value of the coefficient of variation was less than 0.07 for the industries from which these firms were selected. The same procedure was followed to identify the fifty-three firms in the highly volatile industries, except that we started with the highest value of the coefficient of variation, then moved to the next highest value. The final sample consists of fifty-three firms from nine industries that have relatively highly volatile environments. These nine industries had a coefficient of variation of greater than 0.15, at least twice the value of those industries categorized as stable. A listing of the firms in the sample and the coefficient of variation for the firm's industry appear at the end of this appendix.

Measures of Constructs

Prior Firm Financial Performance

This study used two measures of prior firm performance: Altman's Z and return on assets (ROA). The first measure, Altman's Z, is a composite measure that consists of five financial ratios. Although this measure originally was designed as a predictor of bankruptcy for manufacturing firms, it has proven to be a reliable, objective measure of a firm's overall financial well-being (Chakravarthy 1986; Robbins and Pearce 1992).

This measure is calculated as follows:

$$Z = 1.2\,X_i + 1.4\,X_i i + 3.3\,X_i ii + 0.6\,X_i v + 1.0\,X_v$$

where X_i is working capital divided by total assets; $X_i i$ is retained earnings divided by total assets, $X_i ii$ is earnings before interest and taxes divided by total assets; $X_i v$ is the market value of common and preferred stock equity divided by total liabilities; and X_v is sales divided by total assets (Altman 1971). Altman's Z scores were used to classify firms as moving toward bankruptcy if their Z score was below 1.81. If their score was above 2.99, the firm was considered to be healthy.

The second measure of prior firm performance was return on assets (ROA), one of the ratios that is part of the Altman's Z measure. Even though return on assets has many limitations, researchers still consider it to be an important measure of performance (Woo and Willard 1983) and many recent studies on strategic change use it (Lant, Milliken, and Batra 1992; Wiersema and Bantel 1992).

The formula divides each firm's ROA by the average ROA of the firm's primary four-digit SIC classification. This is consistent with the organizational-learning literature, which argues that managers use industry averages as a reference point to assess their performance (Lant, Milliken, and Batra 1992; Grinyer, Mayes, and McKiernan 1988). Following Keats and Hitt (1988), the firm's primary industry was identified by examining the sales distribution of the firm's four-digit SIC codes and selecting the one that accounted for the largest proportion of total firm sales.

An important issue regarding prior performance was to determine how many years needed to be considered in the definition of "prior." Past research has found that firms often experience several periods of declining performance before they consider implementing major changes to their structures and practices (Weitzel and Jonsson 1989). Tushman and Romanelli (1985) have argued that only large or sustained declines in performance are likely to be associated with reorientations. Since most past research that has examined reorientation used three years, for this research a three-year period (1983–1985) was used to examine each firm's prior performance.

For both these measures of prior performance, we used a measure to calculate the relative sharpness of decline in performance. Much of the past research does not include an objective measure of the severity of the decline in prior performance (Robbins and Pearce 1992). Other investigators suggest that the sharper the decline, the less time will pass before the top management team defines a situation as being a crisis and implements major organizational change (Grinyer, Mayes, and McKiernan 1988; Slatter 1984). In this study, we used a measure of relative sharpness of decline in performance. Using both ROA and Altman's Z, we calculated the sum of the difference between 1985 minus 1984 added to 1984 minus 1983.

Stock Ownership

We employed three measures of stock ownership; the proportion of the outstanding stock owned by top management team members, the proportion of stock owned by outside institutions, and a measure of ownership concentration.

Similar to Hill and Snell (1989), we used the percentage of stock controlled directly or indirectly by the firm's top management team members as a measure of inside holdings. For the purposes of this study we defined top management team members as managers who were currently active in the day-to-day operations of the firm and were listed in the firm's proxy report. Stock owned by top management team members' families was considered to be indirectly controlled by those inside managers. This data is available from *Standard & Poor's Stock Guide* and the firm's proxy statements.

A second measure we used concerning the composition of stock ownership was the proportion of total outstanding common stock outside institutions owned. This data was available from Compustat's Industrial Disclosure and the *Standard & Poor's Stock Guide*. Similar to the approach used by Brickley, Lease, and Smith (1988), this study calculated the proportion of the total outstanding stock owned by individual and corporate shareholders of 5 percent or more. This calculation excluded stock held by the firm's managers or their relatives. This information was obtained from the firm's proxy statements.

Board of Directors

The three measures we used to examine the board of directors were the proportion of total directors who were independent of the firm, the average length of tenure of board members, and a measure of the influence of the chief executive officer over the board. In much of the past research, the number of inside directors has been identified based on current or retired corporate officers and relatives of officers. The first measure used in this study was the total number of independent directors on the board divided by the total number of board members. The second measure used was the average tenure of board members (Mallette and Fowler 1992), which we obtained from the firm's proxy statement.

The third measure, the influence of the chief executive officer over the board, was measured by counting the number of directors appointed during the tenure of the chief executive officer, starting with the year after the CEO came to the firm. A count was made of each new director appointed to the board after the first year in which the chief executive officer was appointed. This variable indicates the percentage of new directors in relation to all directors serving during the CEOs' tenure.

Chief Executive Officer

This study used three measures of the characteristics of the chief executive officer: two measures of tenure and a measure concerning the origin of the CEO. The first measure was the length of time the chief executive had been with the firm. This was calculated as the CEO's start date (Mallette and Fowler 1992) subtracted from the year under investigation in the study. The start date was obtained from *Dun & Bradstreet's Reference Book on Corporate Management*. The second measure of tenure was the number of years for which the chief executive had held the current position. Miller (1991) found that CEOs' tenure in their positions was significantly inversely related to the prescribed alignment of strategy with environment. This information also came from *Dun & Bradstreet's Reference Book on Corporate Management*.

The third measure was the origin of the chief executive. We coded a new CEO as being an insider or outsider. Following Virany, Tushman, and Romanelli (1992), this research identified a new chief executive as an outsider if he or she had been employed with the firm for a year or less at the time of being named CEO, and all others were identified as insiders.

Top Management Team

This study used the average tenure of the TMT members to examine the composition of the top management team. Top management team members were defined as including all executives listed as officers of the corporation according to *Dun & Bradstreet's Reference Book on Corporate Management*. We obtained the average tenure of TMT members by subtracting each member's start date with the firm from the year being considered. The data came from *Dun & Bradstreet's Reference Book on Corporate Management*.

Reorientation

This study is interested in the time it takes a firm to initiate a reorientation. Tushman and Romanelli have defined reorientation as "a simultaneous and discontinuous shift in strategy, the distribution of power, the firm's core structure, and the nature and pervasiveness of control systems" (1985, 147).

Two past research studies have operationalized reorientation: by Lant, Milliken, and Batra (1992) and Virany, Tushman, and Romanelli (1992). Both studies examined small, single-product firms. Lant, Milliken, and Batra (1992) operationalized a change in strategy as a change in the description of the firm's means of competing, as given in the firm's 10k report. Virany, Tushman, and Romanelli (1992) operationalized a change in strategy as a change in the products or markets of the firm.

Virany, Tushman, and Romanelli (1992) defined a change in structure as a change in the distribution in the executive team member titles. If one of the categories of titles (functional, geographic, product, or market) reached or dropped below 35 percent of the total number of titles, then the firm was categorized as having had a change in structure. Baumrin (1990) identified a change in structure if there was a change (increase or decrease) in the number of reporting levels in the executive team. Both Lant, Milliken, and Batra (1992) and Virany, Tushman, and Romanelli (1992) agreed that a change had occurred in control systems when a change in inventory control systems, management information systems, manufacturing controls, or management incentive systems was announced.

This study included only large corporations, so we had to identify more clearly corporate-wide changes in these organizational practices. Therefore, the following operational definitions of major corporate change were used:

Corporate Strategy: This study examines larger, multibusiness public corporations that are traded on the New York Stock Exchange, and therefore, a change in strategy is defined as a change in the firm's corporate strategy. Thompson and Strickland (1990) defined corporate strategy as management's overall game plan for its portfolio of businesses. This study will identify a change in corporate strategy as having happened if (1) top management has announced a change in the primary focus of the corporation's business, indicating a shift in corporate investment priorities, and/or, as a result, (2) the corporation has announced acquisitions of new businesses or has divested businesses that no longer fit into current management plans.

Corporate Structure: Similar to past studies, this study seeks evidence to indicate that a major change in the corporate structure has taken place. Evidence of such a change includes (1) a change in the number of reporting levels at the top executive level, such as group or executive vice president (2) if there is an announced restructuring of the corporation in which new divisions have been created or eliminated; and (3) change in primary structure from functional to divisional or to a holding company.

Corporate Control Systems: A change in control systems that was reported in a large corporation's annual report or stock analyst reports is considered to be a significant change to the participants. These could include (1) corporate-wide multiyear quality management programs; (2) new incentive programs for top executives; (3) announced multiyear corporate-wide drives for cost efficiency, just-in-time inventory programs or drives for productivity improvements with announced targets; (4) business units or divisions being reorganized into separate profit/loss centers or companies; and/or (5) change in corporate culture.

The approach that we used to capture organizational change over time was similar to the multistep, multicoding process used by Mintzberg and Waters (1982) and Virany, Tushman and Romanelli (1992). The steps taken were as follows:

Step 1: Histories were compiled for each corporation from 1983 through 1992. These histories are composed of the CEO's letter to stockholders (taken from the annual report), stock analyst reports (Standard & Poor's and Moody's), and any articles listed in Predicast Corporate Change Index and ABI Inform.

Step 2: We reviewed these histories and identified statements that indicated that corporate-wide change had occurred, including only ones that met the definitions given above. Examples of the statements that were obtained are included at the end of this appendix.

Step 3: Two experts in strategic management reviewed a randomly selected group of 40 company histories (out of a total of 100 in the sample). They identified all the statements that they believed were consistent with the operational definitions given above. Out of the 151 statements that we identified, the two experts added 7 statements and deleted 15. In total, there was an 85 percent agreement between reviewers.

Step 4: For all firms in the sample, we placed the statements identified in steps 2 and 3 in coding sheets, examples of which are at the end of this appendix . Four different strategic management experts (not involved in step 2) participated in this step. Each of the 100 sets of firm coding sheets was coded by two of these experts. We asked the experts to use the operational definitions and code the statements as to whether they believed the described change represented a major corporate-wide change or a minor change. If the change was identified as being major, then the expert was asked to code the change as to whether it was a change of strategy, structure, or systems. If there was a disagreement between experts, they reviewed and discussed additional information from the firm's history until they reached agreement.

Since time was the dependent variable in this study and affects our identification of when and whether a reorientation has taken place, no dates were included in the coding sheets. For all 100 firms in the sample, the experts reviewed 377 statements. They were in agreement for 94.2 percent of the cases. Of the 22 disagreements, 14 were disagreements over whether the statement should have been included in two of the categories, such as structure and systems. Only in 8 cases was there a disagreement between categories, and in all of these cases the reviewers came to a quick agreement after an exchange of ideas.

Following Virany, Tushman, and Romanelli (1992), this study measured reorientation as having taken place if, within any two-year period between 1985 and 1991, corporate-wide control systems, structure, and corporate strategy all changed. The time taken to initiate a reorientation is defined as the first year of the two-year period in which the first organizational dimension was changed minus the base year, 1985. For example, for a firm that changed its corporate control systems, structure, and strategy between the years 1987 and 1988, the time it took to initiate a reorientation would be two years. This would be calculated as the first year in which the first dimension changed for a firm that did subsequently experience a reorientation (1987) minus the last year of prior performance examined (1985).

Data Analysis

The analysis of survival data requires that special event history techniques be used. Event history analysis models hazard rates, which express the risk of having an event occur at time t, given that the event did not occur before time t. The occurrence of an event assumes a preceding time interval that represents its nonoccurrence (Yamaguchi 1991).

Event methodology can identify what variables are associated with an increase or decrease of the time interval of nonoccurrence. For this research, the event time methodology estimates the effects of the independent variables (prior performance and participants in the corporate governance structure) on the time it takes before a firm initiates reorientation.

One difficulty with survival data is that the study is often ended at some specified point before the endpoint of the phenomena being studied has been reached. In these cases subjects have survived up to a certain point, beyond which their status is unknown. These cases are known as right censored. One of the major advantages of the hazard rate models used in this research, compared to other linear regression models, is their ability to deal with censored observations (Yamaguchi 1991). This method considers that the observation is censored and weighs the influence of the case accordingly. This is important to this research since the majority of firms (70 percent) did not experience a reorientation during the time period of the study. If only the firms that experienced reorientation were included, this would produce downward-biased estimates of the time periods before the firm experienced reorientation (Mitchell 1989).

Two of the most popular hazard-rate models are the Kalbfleisch and Prentice (1980) model and the Cox proportional hazards model. Most accelerated-failure time models assume a parametric form for the effects of the explanatory variables and a parametric form for the underlying survivor function. The Cox proportional hazard model also assumes a parametric form for the explanatory variables but allows for an unspecified form for the underlying survivor function (SAS Institute 1992).

The specific software package used was SAS PHREG, which performs a regression analysis on the data using the Cox model. The survival time of each member of the population is assumed to follow its own hazard function, hi(t):

$$hi(t) = h(t; z_i) = h_o(t) exp\ (z_i \beta)$$

where $h_0(t)$ is an arbitrary and unspecified baseline hazard function, z_i is the vector of measured explanatory variables, and β is the vector of unknown regression parameters associated with the explanatory variables. A positive coefficient indicates that the independent variable reduces the time to failure, and a negative coefficient indicates that the independent variable increases the time before the failure occurs.

Cox and Oakes (1984) introduced the partial likelihood function, which eliminates the unknown baseline function and accounts for censored survival times. This also allows for time-dependent variables, that is, variables whose value for any given case can change over time (SAS Institute 1992).

The time scale used for the time until the firm initiated reorientation was categorized into years. The PHREG program has the option of using a method to take into account the discrete units. A forward stepwise procedure was used in building the model. An additional advantage of the PHREG program is that it provides a test of the fit of the final model.

FIRMS INCLUDED IN THE SAMPLE

Stable Environment—Low Variability (Coefficient of Variation Less Than 0.07)

SIC 2040—Grain Mill Products (0.0384)
General Mills
Kellogg
Quaker Oats
Ralston Purina

SIC 2060—Sugar and Confectionery Products (0.058)
Hershey Foods
Savannah Foods & Industries
Tootsie Roll Industries
Wrigley (W M.) Jr. Co.

SIC 2080—Beverages (0.066)
Brown-Forman
Coca-Cola
Pepsico
Seagram
Universal Foods

SIC 2330—Women's and Misses' Clothing (0.045)
Kellwood
Liz Claiborne

SIC 2860—Industrial Inorganic Chemicals (0.062)
Crompton & Knowles
Ethyl Corp.
International Flavors & Fragrances
Union Carbide
Witco

SIC 3290—Abrasives (0.064)
Owens-Corning

SIC 3350—Rolling and Draw (0.066)
Handy & Harman

3411—Metal Cans (0.0297)

Ball Corp.
Crown Cork & Seal company
Van Dorn Co.

3420—Cutting, Hand Tools (0.054)
Amdura Corp.
Bairnco Corp.
Gillette company
Snap-On Tools Corp.
Stanley Works

3490—Miscellaneous Fabricated Metal (0.030)
Amcast
ARX
Crane company
Keystone International
Parker-Hannifin

510—Engines and Turbines (0.068)
Briggs & Stratton
Brunswick Corp.
Cummins Engine
McDermott International
Outboard Marine Corp.

SIC 3621—Motors and Generators (0.046)
Baldor Electric
Kollmorgen Corp.
Pacific Scientific Co.

SIC 3861—Photographic Equipment (0.34)
Anacomp
Eastman Kodak
Polaroid Corp.
Xerox

Turbulent Environment—High Variability (Coefficient of Variation Greater than 0.15)

SIC 2911—Oil Refining (0.22)
Amerada Hess Corp.
Ashland Oil Inc.
Atlantic Richfield
Chevron Oil Company
Exxon Corp.
Kerr-Mcgee
Louisiana Land & Exploration

Mapco Inc.
Mobil Oil
Murphy Oil
Pennzoil company
Phillips Petroleum
Quaker State Corp.
Sun company
Tesoro Petroleum
Texaco Inc.
Tosco Corp.
Unocal Corp.
Valero Energy Corp.
Wainco Oil Corp.

SIC 3523—Farm Machinery (0.177)
Allied Products
Deere & company
Tenneco Corp.
Varity Corporation\Massey Ferguson

SIC 3533—Oil Field Equipment (0.35)
Baker-Hughes Inc.
Smith International
Varco International

SIC 3571—Electronic Computers (0.199)
Commodore International
Compaq Computer
Cray Research
Datapoint Computer
Stratus Computer
Tandem Computer

SIC 3724—Aircraft Engines (0.205)
AlliedSignal Inc.
Teledyne Inc.
United Technologies Corp.

SIC 3728—Aircraft Parts (0.165)
Coltec Industries
OEA Inc.
Sundstrand Corp.

SIC 3721—Aircraft (0.1517)
Boeing company
General Dynamics
Grumman Corp.

McDonnell Douglas Corp.
Northrop Corp.

SIC 3760—Guided Missiles (0.1540
GenCorp
Lockheed Corp.
Martin Marietta Corp.
Rockwell International
Thiokol (Morton Thiokol)

SIC 3842—Medical Instruments (0.15)
Bard (C. R.)
Baxter International Inc.
Becton Dickinson & Co.
U.S. Surgical Corp.

INSTRUCTIONS FOR EXPERT CODERS

A. For each of the statements given below, indicate whether you believe that the statement describes a change that is a major, corporate-wide change or a minor change. If the statement meets the operational definition that has been provided you, then the change is to be categorized as a major change. If the statement does not meet the operational definition, then it is to be categorized as a minor statement.

B. Once you have identified the change as being major or minor, then please code the change as to whether it is a change of strategy, structure, systems, or some combination of these.

Operational Definitions of Major Corporate Change

1. *Corporate Strategy*—This study examines larger, multibusiness public corporations that are traded on the New York Stock Exchange. In this study, a change in strategy is defined as a change in the firm's corporate strategy. Thompson and Strickland (1990) defined corporate strategy as management's overall game plan for its portfolio of businesses. This study will identify a change in corporate strategy as having happened if:

   a. top management has announced a change in the primary focus of the corporation's business, indicating a shift in corporate investment priorities, and/or as a result,

   b. the corporation has announced acquisitions of new businesses or has divested businesses that no longer fit into the current managers' plans.

2. *Corporate Structure*—Similar to past studies, this study seeks evidence to indicate that a major change in the corporate structure has taken place. Evidence of such a change includes:

   a. a change in the number of reporting levels at the top executive level, such as group or executive vice president;

   b. an announced restructuring of the corporation in which new divisions have been created or eliminated;

   c. change in primary structure from functional to divisional or to a holding company;

   d. business units or divisions reorganized to be separate profit/loss centers or separate companies.

3. *Corporate Control Systems*—It is argued that any change in control systems that is reported in a large corporation's annual report or stock analyst reports is considered to be a significant change to the participants. Examples of announcements of the following changes were defined as representing major changes to the corporate control systems:

   a. corporate-wide quality management program;

   b. new incentive program for top executives;

   c. announced corporate-wide drive for cost-efficiency;

   d. business units or divisions reorganized to be separate profit/loss centers or separate companies;

   e. change in corporate culture.

Instructions:
A) For each of the statements given below, indicate whether you believe that the statement describes a change that is a major corporate-wide change or a minor change. If the statement meets the operational definition that has been provided then categorize the change as a major change. If the statement does not meet the operational definition then it is to be categorized as a minor change.
B) Once you have identified the change as being major or minor, then please code the change as to whether it is a change of strategy, structure, systems or some combination of these.

Anacomp
Profile: Photographic equipment; micrographics and data services; 1985 sales $123 million

	Minor Change			Major Change		
	Strategy	Structure	Systems	Strategy	Structure	Systems
1) Streamlining organization, cutting employees 25%; sold portions of business						
2) Have made the major decision to develop only new products that are funded from outside sources. Concentrating resources on micrographics operation and innovative software for financial institutions						

3) Executed back to basics plan; "narrower focus on growth in micrographics, consolidation of some operations and sale of certain assets."			
4) Eliminated one of two divisions, divesting banking software and CIS retail banking operations (only micrographics left)			
5) Acquired two related firms in micrographics business with sales of $240 million and $30 million			
6) Acquired related business which had sales of $300 million			

Instructions:

A) For each of the statements given below, indicate whether you believe that the statement describes a change that is a major corporate-wide change or a minor change. If the statement meets the operational definition that has been provided then the change is to be categorized as a major change. If the statement does not meet the operational definition then it is to be categorized as a minor statement.

B) Once you have identified the change as being major or minor, then please code the change as to whether it is a change of strategy, structure, systems or some combination of these.

ARX/Aeroflex Laboratories
Profile: Aerospace; sales were $48 million in 1985.

	Minor Change			Major Change		
	Strategy	Structure	Systems	Strategy	Structure	Systems
1) Reorganized and streamlined our two largest divisions to cut costs and improve future profitability						
2) Cost program put into place to improve company-wide operating margins.						
3) Management and financial resources are to be allocated to grow the commercial/industrial segments (versus government aerospace).						

4) A "major restructuring of business focus...the restructuring has resulted in a smaller, but more focused ARX with emphasis in military electronic and mechanical systems, commercial, industrial and military shock and vibration systems and commercial envelopes." Several non-core businesses divested.	5) "Major restructuring of our operations...to better match our new structure and size, significant reductions in staff and spending levels have been implemented."

Appendix C

Review of the Corporate Governance and Strategic Change Literature

For those readers who are interested in having a better understanding of what academic research has been completed in the area of strategic change and corporate governance, the following literature review is provided.

To begin with, relatively little empirical research has examined the variables associated with the questions of interest to the isues in this book. Recently, there has been an increasing interest in examining the role of different participants in the governance structure on the firm's ability to implement strategic change. However, with the exception of this book, we were unable to identify any research that examines how participants in the broader governance system affect the timeliness in which strategic change or reorientation are initiated.

The following literature review is organized as follows: (1) a review of empirical studies that examined strategic change or reorientations; (2) a review of empirical studies on the time it takes for firms to accomplish major change; (3) a review of the studies that have examined corporate governance and strategic change; and (4) a discussion of the gaps in the current literature.

EMPIRICAL RESEARCH ON REORIENTATION AND STRATEGIC CHANGE

The studies discussed in this section examined factors associated with firms that change strategies or initiate reorientation. Strategy is defined in these studies as a shift in the firm's strategic orientation or a change in the products and services offered by the firm. Examples of some of these recent empirical studies are summarized in Table C.1.

Many of the studies in this section examined only absolute inertia: that is, whether the firms changed their strategies or not during the period of study. These studies provide evidence that the majority of firms were able to make major changes to their organizational practices in response to significant shifts in their respective environments. Examples of these studies include those completed by Smith and Grimm (1987), Hinings and Greenwood (1988), and Zajac and Shortell (1989). The environmental shifts identified in these studies included government deregulation of the railroads, federal government pressure on municipalities to adopt a corporate form of structure, and government change in policies toward hospitals. One can interpret the results of these studies to indicate the strength of inertia forces even in the face of dramatic changes in the respective firms' environments. Roughly 40 percent of the organizations in these studies did not alter their strategies in spite of the presence of tremendous pressures to do so and the passage of three to ten years.

A few studies have specifically examined revolutionary change or reorientation. The first study, completed by Miller and Friesen (1980), proposed a model of adaptation in which the firm experiences periods of momentum and revolution. Revolutionary periods are those in which many strategy and structure variables changed directions over a five-year period. Miller and Friesen (1980) developed twenty different scales to examine different dimensions of a firm's strategy, structure, and systems. These researchers (1984) found that organizations that implemented a complete transformation or reorientation within a short period of time outperformed those organizations that implemented change more gradually.

Virany, Tushman, and Romanelli (1992) operationalized reorientation as having taken place if strategy, structure, and formal controls had all changed within a two-year period. Their model proposed that a firm's subsequent performance was a function of a change in the chief executive officer, a change in executive team, the occurrence of reorientation, and the interaction of these three independent variables. These researchers found that the majority of reorientations occurred after the current chief executive officer had been replaced.

They also found that if firms in turbulent environments made changes to their executive team and implemented reorientations, they enjoyed improved financial performance. The same study also identified a small group of high-performing firms that appeared to initiate reorientations proactively, before the firm's performance had declined. These firms had made no change in their chief executive officer yet were able to

Table C.1
Review of Empirical Research on Strategic Change

AUTHORS	INDUSTRY	CHANGE VARIABLE	ENVIRONMENTAL SHIFT/ PERFORMANCE CHANGE	TIME PERIOD OF STUDY	IMPLICATIONS FOR DEPENDENT VARIABLES
Baumrin (1990)	31 food processors	diversification, TMT, structure	poor performance	2 years following succession	Influence of CEO succession on strategic change influenced by inertia forces and prior performance
Bethel and Liebeskind (1993)	93 Fortune firms	restructuring; portfolio of businesses or capital structure	not addressed	6 years	Found presence of blockholders was related to increased restructuring
Boeker (1989)	51 semi-conductors	generic strategy	turbulent environment	7 years from founding	Founding conditions constrain, poor performance not associated with change
Fombrun and Ginsberg (1990)	352 firms in different industries	strategic orientation - aggressiveness	poor performance and sector volatility	8 years	Found prior performance and sector volatility led to changes in orientation, however infrequent
Ginsberg and Buchholtz (1990)	167 health maintenance organizations (HMOs)	strategic orientation	government policy change	5 years	Inertia and adaptive models explain speed of response

Table C.1 continued

Goodstein and Boeker (1991)	300 hospitals	change in product and services	government policy change	6 years	Changes in ownership, board of directors and CEO associated positively with change
Goodstein, Guatam and Boeker (1994)	334 hospitals	service additions, divestitures and reorganizations	changes in competitive environment	5 years	Diversity of board reduces the amount of strategic change
Haveman (1992)	313 firms	change in diversification	Changes in technology and macro-economic environment	27 years	If change occurs in response to environmental change it was found to enhance the firms ability to survive
Hinings and Greenwood (1988)	27 municipalities	structure	government policy change	10 years	Strength of inertia forces, slowness of response
Johnson, Hoskisson and Hitt (1993)	92 manufacturing firms	restructuring and acquisitions	not addressed	5 years	Board involvement in these decisions influenced by executive tenure and ownership and the proportion of outsiders on the board
Lant, Milliken and Batra (1991)	40 software, 63 furniture	reorientation	prior performance	2 years for change	Performance, CEO, TMT, and managerial interpretations affect the occurrence of reorientation
Romanelli and Tushman (1994)	25 minicomputer firms	reorientation	prior performance and environmental shift	3 years	Environmental change and CEO succession associated with reorientation

Table C.1 continued

Smith and Grimm (1987)	27 railroads	generic strategy	government policy change	5 years	Majority of firms responded and found to perform better than those who did not change
Virany, Tushman and Romanelli (1992)	59 minicomputer firms	reorientation - strategy, structure and control systems	turbulent environment	12 years	CEO and TMT change or TMT change with reorientation associated with improved performance
Zajac and Shortell (1989)	570 hospitals	generic strategy	government policy change	2 years	Found 40 percent had changed, no relationship to performance

127

initiate reorientations before performance declined below the industry average.

The first study that began to identify the determinants of reorientation was completed by Lant, Milliken, and Batra (1992). These researchers operationalized reorientation as a change in business strategy coupled with a change in any other key organizational dimension that occurred within a two-year period of time. These other dimensions included control systems, structure, and power distribution. The researchers measured power distribution in terms of a change in the functional background of the top management team members. The model proposed by Lant, Milliken, and Batra (1992) was that reorientation is determined by prior performance, change in the chief executive officer, change in the top management team, management team heterogeneity, and managerial interpretations. Lant, Milliken, and Batra (1992) found that managers' level of environmental awareness and attributions concerning performance were associated with the likelihood of reorientation. In addition, these researchers found that a change in the chief executive officer or top management heterogeneity was also linked to the likelihood of reorientation and the existence of poor prior performance.

The third study, completed by Romanelli and Tushman (1994), examined a sample of twenty-five minicomputer firms over the period of 1967–1969. These researchers found support for the punctuated equilibrium model, which utilizes the reorientation concept to describe massive organizational change. They found that a large majority of organizational reorientations or transformations were accomplished "via rapid and discontinuous change" (p. 1141). Specifically, these researchers found that firms that implemented more reorientations had experienced a change in chief executive officers and major changes in industry technology.

EMPIRICAL RESEARCH ON TIME TO INITIATE CHANGE

The only major study that was identified as specifically examining the speed of response of organizations to an environmental shift was completed by Ginsberg and Buchholtz (1990). These researchers examined how a sample of 167 HMOs responded to a change in government policies that encouraged HMOs to adopt a for-profit orientation (Ginsberg and Buchholtz 1990). Variables representing inertial and adaptive forces were found to affect the speed of response during which firms changed their strategic orientation.

Although none of the studies listed in Table C.1 specifically examine time with the exception of Ginsberg and Buchholtz (1990), these studies do imply that under certain circumstances, firms can overcome inertia forces and initiate major change relatively quickly. For example, Baumrin (1990) found that under conditions of poor previous firm performance and the presence of a new chief executive officer who came from outside, firms were able to overcome inertia pressures and undergo structural and strategic change. Since Baumrin (1990) only examined the two-year period after succession, this implies that some of the firms did achieve a relatively timely response.

In addition, in an interesting study, Haveman (1992) examined the timing of organizational change in California savings and loan institutions. She found that firms reorienting close to the time when major environmental changes occurred improved their short-term financial performance and the likelihood of their long-term survival. These results suggest that under certain conditions, change can be beneficial, while under others, it can be harmful.

EMPIRICAL RESEARCH ON GOVERNANCE AND STRATEGIC CHANGE

Several researchers (Grinyer, Mayes, and McKiernan 1988; Meyer 1982; Tushman and Romanelli 1985) have identified product life cycles, technology, and changes in the social, political, and legal environment as examples of environmental modifications that cause significant changes within organizations. However, as argued by Geswick (1991), these environmental changes cause a need for organizational change but do not, in themselves, trigger a revolution. Tushman and Romanelli (1985) identified the executive team as the initiators and directors of strategic orientations.

We argue in the model presented in this research that the magnitude of change needed for a reorientation requires decisive action by more than only the firm's executives. Different types of stock owners, members of the board of directors, and top management team members also influence the decision to implement a reorientation. Recently, several researchers have emphasized the importance of the broader governance structure on firm behavior.

Studies completed by Boeker (1989) and Goodstein, Guatam, and Boeker (1994) found evidence concerning the influence of outside directors on the strategic decision-making process in firms during periods of poor performance. Boeker (1989) found that large outside ownership interests influenced the rate and direction of strategic change. Goodstein, Guatam, and Boeker (1994) examined a large sample of hospitals in California over the period of 1980 to 1985. During this period, competition was greatly intensified due to the emergence of new competitors such as health maintenance organizations (HMOs) and preferred provider organizations (PPOs). These researchers found that hospitals that possessed boards with greater diversity initiated less strategic change than homogeneous boards. Board diversity was measured as the degree of differences in occupational backgrounds. This evidence indicates that greater board diversity causes greater conflict within the board, reducing its ability to come to agreement concerning organizational goals and policies. Similarly, an additional study completed by Johnson, Hoskisson, and Hitt (1993) found that board involvement in restructuring decisions was affected by the proportion of outsiders on the board. They also found that if the firm's executives had been employed by the firm for a long time or owned a large amount of stock, then the board tended to be less involved in the strategic decision process.

Last, a study completed by Bethel and Lebeskind (1993) examined the influence of stockholders and firm restructuring. These researchers examined a sample of ninety-three large firms during the period of 1981 to 1987. They found that many firm executives were pressured to restructure their firms as a result of demands from large shareholders. They defined restructuring as changes in the firm's portfolio of businesses or financial structure.

GAPS IN THE CURRENT LITERATURE

The research reported in this book attempts to examine several issues that have not been addressed by the existing literature or that still remain largely unresolved. One issue that has only begun to be addressed in the previous literature is the influence of the broader governance structure. Recently, several researchers have emphasized the importance of political context on that structure (Fredrickson, Hambrick, and Baumrin 1988; Goodstein and Boeker 1991). When analyzing a firm's reorientation, it is important to consider, not only the influence of a new chief executive officer, but also the effect of different types of stock owners, members of the board of directors, and top management team members.

The second issue concerns the type of firms that have been examined in past research on strategic change. Most studies have examined smaller, single-product manufacturing businesses or firms that are in the service sector. However, much evidence in the literature indicates that the strategic change process is very different in larger, multiproduct businesses. For example, in larger organizations, decision making is a shared responsibility (Hambrick and Mason 1984) and such organizations are also more formal and bureaucratic (Child and Kieser 1981), which makes information processing more difficult and slows strategic implementation.

The third issue, which to us is the most important question in strategic management research, concerns the factors that affect the ability of the firm to change in a timely fashion. There appears to be general acceptance in the literature that "organizations tend to demonstrate great sluggishness in adapting to their environments" (Miller and Friesen 1980, 591).

Recently, researchers have expressed an increasing interest in the fourth issue, the importance of time. "Today speed is of the essence. Product life cycles are shorter, development times are getting tighter and customers expect almost instantaneous service" (Hamel and Prahalad 1994, 34). Stalk and Hout (1990) argue that quick response time has become the critical "performance variable" and is often now required for a firm to be able to establish a competitive advantage. However, there appear to be no major empirical research studies that have explored what governance variables are associated with a firm's ability to initiate major change more quickly. This research is one of the first studies to examine what influence participants in the governance structure have on the time it takes a firm to initiate a reorientation.

References

Alderfer, C. P. 1986. The invisible directors on corporate boards. *Harvard Business Review*, 64 (6), 38–50.

Altman, E. 1971. *Corporate Bankruptcy in America*. Lexington, Mass.: Lexington Books, D. C. Heath.

Andrews, K. 1971. *The Concept of Corporate Strategy*. Homewood, Ill.: Dow Jones–Irwin.

Bacon, J. 1990. *Membership and Organization of Corporate Boards*. New York: Conference Board.

Baker, D., and Cullen, J. 1993. Administration reorganization and configurational context: The contingent effects of age, size and change in size. *Academy of Management Journal*, 36, 1251–1277.

Baumrin, S. W. 1990. New CEOs at the helm in large firms: The relationship of the succession context to subsequent organizational change and performance. Unpublished Ph.D. dissertation, Columbia University.

Baysinger, B., and Hoskisson, R. E. 1990. The composition of boards of directors and strategic control: Effects on corporate strategy. *Academy of Management Review*, 15 (1), 72–87.

Baysinger, B., Kosnick, R. D., and Turk, T. A. 1991. Effects of board and ownership structure on corporate R & D strategy. *Academy of Management Journal*, 34 (1), 205–214.

Beam, A., and Dobrzynski, J. A. 1985. General Mills: Toys just aren't us. *Business Week*, September 16, 107–109.

Berle, A., and Means, G. 1932. *The Modern Corporation and Private Property*. New York: Macmillan.

Bethel, J. R., and Liebeskind, J. 1993. The effects of ownership structure on corporate restructuring. *Strategic Management Journal*, 14, 15–31.

Boeker, W. B. 1989. Strategic change: The effects of founding and history. *Academy of Management Journal*, 32, 489–516.

Borrus, Amy. 1994. This is going to be the biggest kahuna around. *Business Week*, September 12, 32.

Brady, G., and Helmich, D. 1984. *Executive Succession*. Englewood Cliffs, N.J.: Prentice-Hall.

Brancato, C. 1993, December. *The Brancato Report on Institutional Investors*. No. 1. Riverside, CA: Riverside Economic Research.

Brickley, J., Lease, R., and Smith, C. 1988. Ownership structure and voting on antitakeover amendments. *Journal of Financial Economics*, 20, 267–291.

Brown, M. C. 1982. Administrative succession and organizational performance: The succession effect. *Administrative Science Quarterly*, 27, 1–16.

Bruner, R., and Brownlee II, E. R. 1990. Leveraged ESOPs, wealth transfers, and shareholder neutrality: The case of Polaroid. *Financial Management*, 19, 59–74.

Chaganti, R., and Damanpour, F. 1991. Institutional ownership, capital structure and firm performance. *Strategic Management Journal*, 12, 479–491.

Chaganti, R., Sherman, H., and Damanpour, F. 1993. The role of institutional investors in corporate governance. In H. Glass, ed., *1994 Handbook of Business Strategy*. New York: Faulkner and Gray.

Chakravarthy, B. 1986. Measuring strategic performance. *Strategic Management Journal*, 5, 437–458.

Chandler, A. 1962. *Strategy and Structure*. Cambridge: MIT Press.

———. 1977. *The Invisible Hand: The Managerial Revolution in American Business*. Cambridge: Harvard University Press.

Child, J., and Kieser, A. 1981. Development of organizations over time. In P. Nystrom, and W. Starbuck, eds., *Handbook of Organizational Design*. New York: Oxford University Press.

Child, J., and Smith, C. 1987. The context and process of organizational transformation: Cadbury Ltd. *Journal of Management*, 24, 565–594.

Cox, D., and Oakes, D. 1984. *Analysis of Survival Data*. London: Chapman and Hall.

Cyert, R., and March, J. 1963. *A Behavioral Theory of the Firm*. Englewood Cliffs, N.J.: Prentice-Hall.

Dalton, D., and Kesner, I. 1983. Inside/outside succession and organizational size: The pragmatics of executive replacement. *Academy of Management Journal*, 26, 736–742.

D'Aveni, R. 1994. *Hypercompetition: Managing the Dynamics of Strategic Maneuvering*. New York: Free Press.

Demsetz, H. 1983. The structure of ownership and the theory of the firm. *Journal of Law and Economics*, 20, 267–291.

Deveny, K. 1986. How Baxter Travenol is treating its digestion problems. *Business Week*, November 10, 69–70.

Dobrzynski, J. 1987. Will all that restructuring ever pay off for Ed Hennessy's Allied? *Business Week*, February 2, 78–80.

– – – . 1990. Lockheed's lesson: It's open season on yes-man boards. *Business Week*, April 16, 25.

Donaldson, G. 1994. *Corporate Restructuring: Managing the Change Process from Within*. Boston, Mass.: Harvard Business School Press.

Drucker, P. 1991. Reckoning with the Pension Fund Revolution. *Harvard Business Review*, March–April 106–9, 111.

Eisenhardt, K. 1989. Making fast strategic decisions in high velocity environments. *Academy of Management Journal*, 32, 543–576.

Fama, E. F. 1980. Agency problems and the theory of the firm. *Journal of Political Economy*, 88, 288–307.

Finkelstein, S., and Hambrick, D. 1990. Top management tenure and organizational outcomes: The moderating role of managerial discretion. *Administrative Science Quarterly*, 35, 484–503.

Flynn, Siler. 1990. Will another round of surgery help Baxter? *Business Week*, April 30, 92.

Fombrun, C. J., and Ginsberg, A. 1990. Shifting gears: Enabling change in corporate aggressiveness. *Strategic Management Journal*, 11, 297–308.

Frank, R. 1996. Pepsico critics fear glass half empty. *Wall Street Journal*, September 30, B4.

Fredrickson, J., Hambrick, D., and Baumrin, S. 1988. A model of CEO dismissal. *Academy of Management Journal*, 13, 255–270.

Friedman, S., and Singh, H. 1989. CEO succession and stakeholder reaction. *Academy of Management Journal*, 32, 718–744.

Fromson, B. 1990. The big owners roar. *Fortune*, July 30, 66–78.

Geswick, C. G. 1991. Revolutionary change theories: A multilevel exploration of the punctuated equilibrium paradigm. *Academy of Management Review*, 16, 10–36.

Ginsberg, A., and Buchholtz, A. 1990. Converting to for-profit status: Corporate responsiveness to radical change. *Academy of Management Journal*, 33, 445–477.

Goodstein, J., and Boeker, W. 1991. Turbulence at the top: A new perspective ongovernance structure changes and strategic change. *Academy of Management Journal*, 34 (2), 300–330.

Goodstein, J., Gautam, K., and Boeker, W. 1994. The effects of board size and diversity on strategic change. *Strategic Management Journal*, 15, 241–250.

Gould, S. J. 1989. Punctuated equilibrium in fact and theory. *Journal of Social Biological Structure*, 12, 117–136.

Graves, S., and Waddock, S. 1990. Institutional ownership' and corporate control. *Academy of Management Executive*, 4, 75–83.

Graves, S. B. 1988. Institutional ownership and corporate R & D in the computer industry. *Academy of Management Journal*, 31, 417–428.

Grinyer, P., Mayes, D., and McKiernan, P. 1988. *Sharpbenders: The Secrets of Unleashing Corporate Potential*. London: Basil Blackwell.

Grinyer, P., and McKiernan, P. 1990. Generating major change in stagnating companies. *Strategic Management Journal*, 11, 131–146.

Hambrick, D., and Fukutomi, G. D. 1991. The seasons of a CEO's tenure. *Academy of Management Review*, 16 (4), 719–742.

Hambrick, D., and Mason, P. 1984. Upper echelons: The organization as a reflection of its top managers. *Academy of Management Review*, 9, 193–200.

Hamel, G., and Prahalad, C. K. 1994. *Competing for the Future*. Boston: Harvard Business School Press.

Hammonds, K. 1988. Why Polaroid must remake itself—Instantly. *Business Week*, September 19, 66–72.

Hannan, M. T., and Freeman, J. H. 1984. Structural inertia and organizational change. *American Sociological Review*, 49, 149–164.

Hansen, G. S., and Hill, C. W. 1991. Are institutional investors myopic? A time-series study of four technology-driven industries. *Strategic Management Journal*, 12, 1–16.

Harrison, R. 1987. The strategic use of corporate board committees. *California Management Review*, Fall, 109–125.

Haveman, H. A. 1992. Between a rock and a hard place: Organizational change and performance under conditions of fundamental environmental transformation. *Administrative Science Quarterly*, 37, 48–75.

Herman, E. S. 1981. *Corporate Control: Corporate Power.* New York: Cambridge University Press.

Hill, C. W., and Snell, S. A. 1989. Effects of ownership structure and control on corporate productivity. *Academy of Management Journal,* 32 (1), 25–46.

Hinings, C. R., and Greenwood, R. 1988. *The Dynamics of Strategic Change.* New York: Basil Blackwell.

Ingrassia, P., and White, J. R. 1994. *Comeback: The fall and rise of the American automobile industry.* New York: Simon and Schuster.

Jarrell, G., Lehn, K., and Marr, W. 1985. Institutional Ownership, Tender Offers and Long Term Investments, Washington, D.C.: Office of the Chief Economist Securities and Exchange Commission.

Jensen, M., and Murphy, K. 1990. CEO incentives—It's not how much you pay, but how. *Harvard Business Review,* May-June, 138–153.

Johnson, R., Hoskisson, R., and Hitt, M. 1993. Board of director involvement in restructuring: The effects of board versus managerial controls and characteristics. *Strategic Management Journal,* 14, 33–50.

Kalbfleisch, J., and Prentice, R. 1980. *The Statistical Analysis of Failure Time Data.* New York: Wiley.

Keats, B., and Hitt, M. 1988. A causal model of linkages among environmental dimensions: Macro-organizational characteristics and performance. *Academy of Management Journal,* 31, 570–597.

Kelly, K. 1994. A CEO who kept his eye on the prize. *Business Week,* August 1, 32.

Kochar, R., and David, P. 1996. Institutional investors and firm innovation: A test of competing hypotheses. *Strategic Management Journal,* 17, 73–84.

Lant, T. K., Milliken, F., and Batra, B. 1992. The role of managerial learning and interpretation in strategic persistence and reorientation: An empirical exploration. *Strategic Management Journal,* 13, 585–608.

Lawrence, P., and Lorsch, J. 1967. *Organization and Environment.* Cambridge: Harvard University Press.

Leinster, C. 1985. Allied-Signal's tough skipper. *Fortune,* June 24, 90–94.

Levy, A. 1986. Second order planned change: Definition and conceptualization. *Organizational Dynamics,* 15 (Summer): 5–20.

Light, L., and Tilsner, J. 1993. Genius watch: Decoding the software King. *Business Week*, October 18, 64–65.

Lorsch, J. W. 1989. *Pawns or potentates: The reality of America's corporate boards*. Boston: Harvard Business School Press.

Lowenstein, L. 1991. Why managers should and should not have respect for their shareholders. *Journal of Corporation Law*, 17, 1–27.

Mace, M. L. 1971. *Directors: Myth and reality*. Cambridge: Harvard Business School.

Mallette, P., and Fowler, K. 1992. Effects of board composition and stock ownership on the adoption of "poison pills." *Academy of Management Journal*, 35, 1010–1035.

Mehler, M. 1985. Nagging problems for the other GM. *Financial World*, January 9–22, 84–85.

Meyer, A. 1982. Adapting to environmental jolts. *Administrative Science Quarterly*, 27, 515–537.

Meyer, R. 1988. The final straw. *Financial World*, January 26, 39–40.

Miles, R. E., and Snow, C. C. 1978. *Organizational Strategy, Structure and Process*. New York: McGraw-Hill.

Miller, D. 1991. Stale in the saddle: CEO tenure and the match between organization and environment. *Management Science*, 37 (1), 34–52.

Miller, D., and Friesen, P. H. 1978. Archetypes of strategy formulation. *Management Science*, 24, 921–933.

———. 1980. Momentum and revolution in organizational adaptation. *Academy of Management Journal*, 22, 591–614.

———. 1984. *Organizations: A Quantum View*. Englewood Cliffs, N.J.: Prentice-Hall.

Milliken, F. J., and Lant, T. K. 1991. The effect of an organization's recent history on strategic persistence and change: The role of managerial interpretations. In J. Dutton, A. Huff, and P. Shrivastava, eds., *Advances in Strategic Management*, vol. 7. Greenwich: JAI Press, 125–152.

Mintzberg, H. 1978. Patterns in strategy formation. *Management Science*, 24, 934–948.

———. 1983. *Power in and around Organizations*. Englewood Cliffs, N.J.: Prentice-Hall.

Mintzberg, H., and Waters, J. 1982. Tracking strategy in an entrepreneurial firm. *Academy of Management Journal*, 25, 465–499.

Mitchell, W. 1989. Whether and when? Probability and timing of incumbents' entry into emerging industrial subfields. *Administrative Science Quarterly*, 34, 208–240.

Mizruchi, M. 1983. Who controls whom? An examination of the relation between management and the board of directors in large U.S. corporations. *Academy of Management Review*, 8, 426–435.

Mizruchi, M., and Stearns, L. 1988. A longitudinal study of the formation of interlocking directorates. *Administrative Science Quarterly*, 33, 194–210.

Monks, R., and Minow, N. 1995. *Corporate Governance*. Cambridge: Basil Blackwell.

———. 1996. *Watching the Watchers: Corporate Governance for the 21st Century*. Cambridge: Basil Blackwell.

Nadler, D., Shaw, R., and Walton, A. 1995. *Discontinuous Change: Leading Organizational Transformations*. San Francisco: Jossey-Bass.

National Association of Corporate Directors (NACD). 1994. *Blue Ribbon Commission Report on Performance Evaluation of CEOs, Boards, and Directors*. Washington, D.C.: NACD.

Norman, James R. 1985. The sharks keep circling Phillips. *Business Week*, February 11, 24–25.

———. 1986. What the raiders did to Phillips Petroleum. *Business Week*. March 17, 102–103.

Nussbaum, B., and Dobryznski, J. H. 1987. The battle for corporate control. *Business Week*, May 18, 102–109.

Nystrom, P. C., and Starbuck, W. H. 1984. To avoid organizational crises—Unlearn. *Organizational Dynamics*, 12 (4), 53–65.

Oswald, S., and Jahera, J. 1991. The influence of ownership on performance: An empirical study. *Strategic Management Journal*, 12, 321–326.

Palmer, J. 1991. Spending Kodak's money: Polaroid uses its settlement bounty to sow seeds of future growth. *Barron's*, October 7, 16–17.

Parker, M. 1990. Lockheed eyes board nomination changes. *Pensions and Investments*, June 11, 29.

Parker, M., and Givant, M. 1987. Executives warned of proxy vote liability. *Pensions and Investment Age*, 15 (May): 53–58.

Patton, A., and Baker, J. C. 1987. Why won't directors rock the boat? *Harvard Business Review*, November-December, 10–17.

Pettigrew, A. 1985. *The Awakening Giant: Continuity and Change in Imperial Chemical Industries*. Oxford: Basil Blackwell.

Pfeffer, J. 1972. Size and the composition of corporate boards of directors: The organization and its environment. *Administrative Science Quarterly*, 17, 218–227.

———. 1981. *Power in Organizations*. Marshfield, Mass.: Pittman.

— — —. 1986. A resource dependence perspective on intercorporate relations. In M. Mizruchi and M. Schwartz, eds., *Structural Analysis of Business*. New York: Harper and Row.

Pfeffer, J., and Salancik, G. 1978. *The External Control of Organizations*. New York.: Harper and Row.

Picker, I. 1989. I. M. (Mac) Booth of Polaroid: The ESOP solution. *Institutional Investor*, September, 87–88.

Porter, M. 1980. *Competitive Strategy*. New York: The Free Press.

Rice, F. 1989. The other Disney in the spotlight. *Fortune*, June 5, 161–168.

Robbins, D., and Pearce, J. 1992. Turnaround, retrenchment and recovery. *Strategic Management Journal*, 13, 287–309.

Romanelli, E., and Tushman, M. L. 1994. Organizational transformation as punctuated equilibrium: An empirical test. *Academy of Management Journal,* 37, 1141–1166.

Rublin, L. 1984. Phillips pays the price—and T. Boone Pickens makes another big score. *Barron's*, December 31, 13, 31.

— — —. 1991. Just what the doctor ordered: Baxter plus American hospital equals a robust competitor. *Barron's*, December 1, 3, 20–24.

Sahal, J. 1981. *Patterns of Technological Innovation*. Reading, Mass.: Harvard University Press.

Salancik, G. 1977. Commitment and the control of organizational behavior and belief. In B. Staw and G. Salancik, eds., *New Directions in Organizational Behavior*. Chicago: St. Clair Press, pp. 1–54.

SAS Institute. 1992. *SAS Technical Report: P–229*. N.C.: Author.

Schine, E. 1989. Lockheed dons new armor to keep the raiders at bay. *Business Week*, April 17, 20–21.

— — —. 1993. Lockheed sticks to its guns. *Business Week*, April 26, 100–102.

Shapiro, E. 1996. Viacom resists spinning off Blockbuster and weighs servicing PC's. *Wall Street Journal*, October 3, B5.

Sherman, H., Beldona, S., and Joshi, M. 1996, November. Institutional investors: Four distinctive types. In M. Schnake, ed., *Southern Management Association*. New Orleans: Southern Management Association, pp. 7–10.

Slatter, S. 1984. *Corporate Recovery: Successful Turnaround Strategies and Their Implementation*. Harmondsworth, U.K.: Penguin.

Smith, K., and Grimm, C. 1987. Environmental variation, strategic change and firm performance: A study of railroad deregulation. *Strategic Management Journal*, 8, 363–376.

Staff. 1997. Larry Bossidy won't stop pushing. *Fortune*, 135, January 11, 135–139.

Stalk, G., and Hout, T. 1990. *Competing against Time: How Time Based Competition Is Reshaping Global Markets*. New York: Free Press.

Star, M. 1993. Sears resolution gains support. *Pensions and Investments*, May 3, 46.

Starbuck, W., and Hedberg, B. 1977. Saving an organization from a stagnating environment. In H. Thorelli, ed., *Strategy + Structure = Performance*. Bloomington: Indiana University Press.

Staw, B. M. 1981. The escalation of commitment to a course of action. *Academy of Management Review*, 6, 577–587.

Staw, B. M., Sandelands, L., and Dutton, J. 1981. Threat rigidity effects in organizational behavior: A multilevel analysis. *Administrative Science Quarterly*, 31, 439–465.

Stewart, T. 1992. Allied-Signal's turnaround blitz. *Fortune*, November 30, 72–76.

———. 1993. The King is dead. *Fortune*, 127, January 11, 34–37.

Taylor, W. 1990. Can big owners make a big difference? *Harvard Business Review*, September–October, 70–82.

Therrien, L. 1988. Mr. Rust Belt. *Business Week*, October 17, 72–79.

Thompson, A., and Strickland, A. 1990. *Strategic Management: Concepts and Cases*. Homewood, Ill.: Irwin.

Tichy, N., and Ulrich, D. 1984. Revitalizing organizations: The leadership role. In J. Kimberly and R. Quinn, eds., *Managing Organizational Transitions*. Homewood, Ill.: Richard Irwin.

Toffler, A. 1990. Toffler's next shock. *World Monitor*, 16, 6–10.

Tushman, M. L., Newman, W. H., and Romanelli, E. 1986. Convergence and upheaval: Managing the unsteady pace of organizational evolution. *California Management Review*, 29 (1), 29–44.

Tushman, M. L., and Romanelli, E. 1985. Organizational evolution: A metamorphosis model of convergence and reorientation. In L. L. Cummings and B. W. Staw, eds., *Research in Organizational Behavior*, vol. 7. Greenwich: JAI Press, pp. 171–222.

Useem, M. 1993. *Executive Defense: Shareholder Power and Corporate Reorganization*. Cambridge: Harvard University Press.

Vance, S. C. 1983. *Corporate leadership: Boards, directors and strategy*. New York.: McGraw-Hill.

Vancil, R. F. 1987. *Passing the baton: Managing the process of CEO succession*. Boston: Harvard Business School Press.

Virany, B., Tushman, M., and Romanelli, E. 1992. Executive succession and organization outcomes in turbulent environments: An organizational learning approach. *Organizational Science*, 3, 72–91.

Waldo, C. N. 1985. *Boards of directors: Their changing roles, structures and information needs*. Westport, Conn.: Quorum Books.

Weitzel, W., and Jonsson, E. 1989. Decline in organizations: A literature integration and extension. *Administrative Science Quarterly*, 34, 91–109.

Wiersema, M. F., and Bantel, K. A. 1992. Top management team demography and corporate strategic change. *Academy of Management Journal*, 35, 91–121.

Woo, C., and Willard, W. 1983. Performance representations in business policy research: Discussion and recommendations. Paper presented at the 23rd National Academy of Management conference, Boston, Mass. August.

Wrubel, R. 1989. Rape and pillage in Burbank. *Financial World*, April 18, 66–67.

Yamaguchi, K. 1991. *Event History Methodology*. Newbury, Calif.: Sage.

Zajac, E. J., and Shortell, S. M. 1989. Changing generic strategies: Likelihood, direction and performance implications. *Strategic Management Journal*, 10, 413–430.

Zald, M. N. 1969. The power and function of boards of directors: A theoretical synthesis. *American Journal of Sociology*, 75, 1073–1119.

Zellner, W., and Rothman, A. 1992. The airline mess. *Business Week*, July 6, 50.

Selected Bibliography

For readers who would like to read more on this subject, a selected readings list has been provided below; it is organized by the major topics that were discussed in this book.

THE CHIEF EXECUTIVE OFFICER AND TOP MANAGEMENT TEAM

Baumrin, S. W. "New CEOs at the Helm in Large Firms: The Relationship of the Succession Context to Subsequent Organizational Change and Performance." Unpublished Ph.D. dissertation, Columbia University, 1990.

Beatty, R., and E. Zajac. "CEO Change and Firm Performance in Large Corporations: Succession Effects and Manager Effects." *Strategic Management Journal,* 8 (1987): 305–318.

Boeker, W. "Strategic Change: The Influence of Managerial Characteristics and Organizational Growth." *Academy of Management Journal,* 40 (1997): 152–170.

Finkelstein, S., and D. Hambrick. "Top Management Tenure and Organizational Outcomes: The Moderating Role of Managerial Discretion." *Administrative Science Quarterly,* 35 (1990): 484–503.

———. *Strategic Leadership: Top Executives and Their Effect on Organizations.* St. Paul: West, 1996.

Gabarro, J. J. *The Dynamics of Taking Charge*. Boston: Harvard Business School Press, 1987.

Haleblian, J., and S. Finkelstein. "Top Management Team Size, CEO Dominance, and Firm Performance: Role of Environmental Turbulence and Discretion." *Academy of Management Journal*, 36 (1993): 844–863.

Hambrick, D. *The Executive Effect: Concepts and Methods for Studying Top Managers*. Greenwich, Conn.: JAI Press, 1988.

Hambrick, D., and G. Fukutomi. "The Seasons of a CEO's Tenure." *Academy of Management Review*, 16, no. 4 (1991): 719–742.

Hambrick, D., M. Geletkanycz, and J. Fredrickson. "Top Executive Commitment to the Status Quo: Some Tests of Its Determinants." *Strategic Management Journal*, 14 (1993): 401–418.

Hickson, D., R. Butler, G. Mallory, D. Cray, and D. Wilson. *Top Decisions: Strategic Decision Making in Organizations*. San Francisco: Jossey-Bass, 1986.

Kotter, J. P. *The General Managers*. New York: Free Press, 1982.

McEachern, W. A. *Managerial Control and Performance*. Lexington, Mass.: Lexington Books, 1975.

Michel, J., and D. Hambrick. "Diversification Posture and Top Management Team Characteristics." *Academy of Management Journal*, 35 (1992): 9–37.

Miller, D. "Stale in the Saddle: CEO Tenure and the Match between Organization and Environment." *Management Science*, 37 no. 1 (1991): 34–52.

Rechner, P., and D. Dalton. "CEO Duality and Organizational Performance: A Longitudinal Analysis " *Strategic Management Journal*, 12 (1991): 155–160.

Wiersema, M. F., and K. Bantel. "Top Management Team Demography and Corporate Strategic Change." *Academy of Management Journal*, 35 (1992): 91–121.

BOARD OF DIRECTORS

Alderfer, C. P. "The Invisible Directors on Corporate Boards." *Harvard Business Review*, 64, no. 6 (1986): 38–50.

Bacon, J. *Membership and Organization of Corporate Boards*. New York: Conference Board, 1990.

Bacon, J., and J. Brown. *Corporate Directorship Practices*. New York: Conference Board, 1975.

Baysinger, B., and H. Butler. "Corporate Governance and the Board of Directors: Performance Effects of Changes in Board Composition." *Journal of Law, Economics, and Organizations*, 1 (1985): 101–124.

Baysinger, B., and R. Hoskisson. "The Composition of Boards of Directors and Strategic Control: Effects on Corporate Strategy." *Academy of Management Review*, 15, no. 1 (1990): 72–87.

Baysinger, B., R. Kosnick, and T. Turk. "Effects of Board and Ownership Structure on Corporate R and D Strategy." *Academy of Management Journal*, 34, no. 1 (1991): 205–214.

Boeker, W., and J. Goodstein. "Organizational Performance and Adaptation: Effects of Environment and Performance on Changes in Board Composition." *Academy of Management Journal*, 34 (1991): 805–826.

– – –. "Performance and Successor Choice: The Moderating Effects of Governance and Ownership." *Academy of Management Journal*, 36 (1993): 172–186.

Cochran, P., R. Wood, and T. Jones. "The Composition of Boards of Directors and Incidence of Golden Parachutes." *Academy of Management Journal*, 28 (1985): 664–671.

Demb, A., and F. Neubauer. *The Corporate Board: Confronting the Paradoxes*. Oxford: Oxford University Press, 1992.

Donaldson, G. "A New Tool for Boards: The Strategic Audit." *Harvard Business Review*, July–August 1995, 99–107.

Goodstein, J., K. Gautam, and W. Boeker. "The Effects of Board Size and Diversity on Strategic Change." *Strategic Management Journal*, 15 (1994): 241–250.

Hermalin, B., and M. Weisbach. "The Determinants of Board Composition." *Rand Journal of Economics*, 19 (1988): 589–606.

Johnson, E. "An Insider's Call for Outside Direction." *Harvard Business Review*, March–April 1990: 46–55.

Johnson, R., R. Hoskisson, and M. Hitt. "Board of Director Involvement in Restructuring: The Effects of Board versus Managerial Controls and Characteristics." *Strategic Management Journal*, 14 (1993): 33–50.

Jones, T. M. and L. D. Goldberg. "Governing the Large Corporation: More Arguments for Public Directors." *Academy of Management Review*, 7 (1982): 603–611.

Judge, W., and C. Zeithaml. "Institutional and Strategic Choice Perspectives on Board Involvement in the Strategic Decision Process." *Academy of Management Journal*, 35 (1992): 766–794.

Kesner, I. "Directors' Characteristics and Committee Membership: An Investigation of Type, Tenure, and Gender." *Academy of Management Journal*, 31 (1988): 66–84.

Lorsch, J. "Empowering the Board." *Harvard Business Review,* January–February 1995, 107–117.

Lorsch, J., and E. MacIver. *Pawns or Potentates: The Reality of America's Corporate Boards.* Boston: Harvard Business School Press, 1989.

Mallette, P., and K. Fowler. "Effects of Board Composition and Stock Ownership on the Adoption of 'Poison Pills.'" *Strategic Management Journal,* 35 (1992): 1010–1035.

Mattar, E., and M. Ball. *Handbook for Corporate Directors.* New York: McGraw-Hill, 1985.

Milles, G. *On the Board.* London: Gower Publishing Ltd., 1981.

Mizruchi, M. "Who Controls Whom? An Examination of the Relation between Management and the Board of Directors in Large U.S. Corporations." *Academy of Management Review,* 8 (1983): 426–435.

Mizruchi, M., and L. Stearns. "A Longitudinal Study of the Formation of Interlocking Directorates." *Administrative Science Quarterly,* 33 (1988): 194–210.

Pearce, J., and S. Zahra. "Board Composition from a Strategic Contingency Perspective." *Journal of Management Studies,* 29 (1992): 412–438.

Pfeffer, J. "Size and the Composition of Corporate Boards of Directors: The Organization and Its Environment." *Administrative Science Quarterly,* 17 (1972): 218–129.

Stearns, L., and M. Mizruchi. "Board Composition and Corporate Financing: The Impact of Financial Institution Representation on Borrowing." *Academy of Management Journal,* 36 (1993): 603–618.

Vance, S. C. *Corporate Leadership: Boards, Directors and Strategy.* New York: McGraw-Hill, 1983.

Waldo, C. N. *Boards of Directors: Their Changing Roles, Structures and Information Needs.* Westport, Conn.: Quorum Books, 1985.

Working Group on Corporate Governance. "A New Compact for Owners and Directors." *Harvard Business Review,* July–August 1991, 142–143.

Zahra, S., and J. Pearce. "Boards of Directors and Corporate Financial Performance: A Review and Integrative Model." *Journal of Management,* 15 (1989): 291–344.

INSTITUTIONAL OWNERS

Barnard, J. "Institutional Investors and the New Corporate Governance." *North Carolina Law Review,* 69 (1991): 1135–1187.

Biersach, J. *Voting By Institutional Investors on Corporate Governance Issues in the 1990 Proxy Season*. Washington, D.C.: Investor Responsibility Research Center, 1990.

Black, B. "Agents Watching Agents: The Promise of Institutional Investor Voice." *UCLA Law Review*, 39 (1992): 811–893.

———. "The Value of Institutional Monitoring: The Empirical Evidence." *UCLA Law Review*, 3 (1992): 896–893.

Blasi, J., and D. Kruse. *The New Owners: The Mass Emergence of Employee Ownership in Public Companies and What It Means to American Business*. New York: Harper Business, 1991.

Brancato, C. *The Brancato Report on Institutional Investors*. No. 1. Riverside, CA: Riverside Economic Research (Dec. 1993).

Brancato, C., and P. Gaughan. *The Growth of Institutional Investors in U.S. Capital Markets: Updated Data 1981–88*. New York: Columbia University Institutional Investor Project, 1990.

Campbell, J., and L. Lindberg. "The Evolution of Governance Regimes." In *Governance in the American Economy*, edited by John Campbell, J. Hollingsworth, and L. Lindberg. New York: Cambridge University Press, 1991.

Chaganti, R., H. Sherman, and F. Damanpour. "The Role of Institutional Investors in Corporate Governance." In *1994 Handbook of Business Strategy*, edited by H. Glass. New York: Faulkner and Gray, 1993.

Drucker, P. *The Unseen Revolution: How Pension Fund Socialism Came to America*. New York: Harper and Row, 1976.

———. "Reckoning with the Pension Fund Revolution." *Harvard Business Review*, March–April 1991: 106–111.

Graves, S. B. "Institutional Ownership and Corporate R&D in the Computer Industry." *Academy of Management Journal*, 31 (1988): 417–428.

Graves, S., and S. Waddock. "Institutional Ownership and Control: Implications for Long Term Corporate Strategy." *Academy of Management Executive*, 4 (1990): 75–83.

———. "Institutional Owners and Corporate Social Performance." *Academy of Management Journal*, 37 (1994): 1034–1046.

Hansen, G. S., and C. W. Hill. "Are Institutional Investors Myopic? A Time-series Study of Four Technology Driven Industries." *Strategic Management Journal*, 12 (1991): 1–16.

Jarrell, G., K. Lehn, and W. Marr. *Institutional Ownership, Tender Offers and Long Term Investments*. Washington, D.C.:, Securities and Exchange Commission, Office of the Chief Economist 1985.

Kochar, R., and P. David. "Institutional Investors and Firm Innovation: A Test of Competing Hypotheses." *Strategic Management Journal,* 17 (1996): 73–84.

National Association of Corporate Directors (NACD). *NACD 1992 Corporate Governance Survey.* Washington, D.C.: Author, 1992.

O'Barr, W., and J. Conley. *Fortune and Folly: The Wealth and Power of Institutional Investing.* Homewood, Ill.: Business One Irwin, 1992.

Roe, M. "The Modern Corporation and Private Pensions." *UCLA Law Review,* 41 (1993): 1.

GENERAL READINGS ON CORPORATE GOVERNANCE

Berle, A., and G. Means. *The Modern Corporation and Private Property.* New York: Macmillan, 1932.

Daily, C. "Governance Patterns in Bankruptcy Reorganizations." *Strategic Management Journal,* 17 (1996): 355–375.

Daily, C., and D. Dalton. "Corporate Governance and the Bankrupt Firm: An Empirical Assessment." *Strategic Management Journal,* 15 (1994): 643–654.

Fligstein, N. *The Transformation of Corporate Control.* Cambridge: Harvard University Press, 1990.

Gilson, S. "Bankruptcy, Boards, Banks and Blockholders." *Journal of Financial Economics,* 26 (1990): 355–387.

Goodstein, J., and W. Boeker. "Turbulence at the Top: A New Perspective on Governance Structure Changes and Strategic Change." *Academy of Management Journal,* 34, no. 2 (1991): 306–330.

Jensen, M. "Eclipse of the Public Corporation." *Harvard Business Review,* May–June 1989 138–153.

Jensen, M., and J. Warner. "The Distribution of Power among Corporate Managers, Shareholders and Directors." *Journal of Financial Economics,* 20 (1989): 3–24.

McWhirter, D. *Sharing Ownership.* New York: John Wiley and Sons, 1993.

———. *Ownership and Control: Rethinking Corporate Governance for the Twenty-First Century.* Washington, D.C.: Brookings Institution, 1995.

Mintzberg, H. *Power in and around Organizations.* Englewood Cliffs, N.J.: Prentice-Hall, 1983.

Monks, R., and N. Minow. *Corporate Governance.* Cambridge: Basil Blackwell, 1995.

Pearce, J., and S. Zahra. "The Relative Power of CEOs and Boards of Directors: Associations with Corporate Performance." *Strategic Management Journal*, 12 (1991): 135–153.

Pfeffer, J. *Power in Organizations*. Marshfield, Mass.: Pittman, 1981.

Pfeffer, J., and G. Salancik. *The External Control of Organizations*, New York: Harper and Row, 1978.

Pound, J. "The Promise of the Governed Corporation." *Harvard Business Review*, March–April 1995, 89–98.

Rediker, K., and A. Seth. "Boards of Directors and Substitution Effects of Alternative Governance Mechanisms." *Strategic Management Journal*, 16 (1995): 85–99.

Useem, M. *Executive Defense: Shareholder Power and Corporate Reorganization*. Cambridge: Harvard University Press, 1993.

LARGE SHAREHOLDERS

Brickley, J., R. Lease, and C. Smith. "Ownership Structure and Voting on Antitakeover Amendments." *Journal of Financial Economics*, 20 (1988): 267–291.

Cubbin, J., and D. Leech. "The Effect of Shareholding Dispersion on the Degree of Control in British Companies: Theory and Measurement." *Economic Journal*, 93 (1983): 351–369.

Pound, J. "Proxy Contests and the Efficiency of Shareholder Oversight." *Journal of Financial Economics*, 20 (January/March 1988): 237–265.

Shleifer, A., and R. Vishny. "Large Shareholders and Corporate Control." *Journal of Political Economy*, 94 (1986): 461–488.

Taylor, W. "Can Big Owners Make a Big Difference?" *Harvard Business Review*, September–October 1990, 70–82.

REORIENTATION AND RESTRUCTURING

Champy, J., and N. Nohria. *Fast Forward: The Best Ideas on Managing Business Change*. Boston: Harvard Business School Press, 1996.

D'Aveni, R. *Hypercompetition: Managing the Dynamics of Strategic Maneuvering*. New York: Free Press, 1994.

Fombrun, C. J., and A. Ginsberg. "Shifting Gears: Enabling Change in Corporate Aggressiveness." *Strategic Management Journal*, 11 (1990): 297–308.

Grinyer, P., D. Mayes, and P. McKiernan. *Sharpbenders: The Secrets of Unleashing Corporate Potential*. London: Basil Blackwell, 1988.

Grinyer, P., and P. McKiernan. "Generating Major Change in Stagnating Companies." *Strategic Management Journal,* 11 (1990): 131–146.

Hambrick, D., and R. D'Aveni. "Large Corporate Failures as Downward Spirals." *Administrative Science Quarterly,* 33 (1988): 1–23.

Hamel, G., and C. K. Prahalad. *Competing for the Future.* Boston: Harvard Business School Press, 1994.

Haveman, H. "Between a Rock and a Hard Place: Organizational Change and Performance under Conditions of Fundamental Environmental Transformation." *Administrative Science Quarterly,* 37 (1992): 48–75.

Hoskisson, R. E., R. Johnson, and D. Moesel. "Corporate Divestiture Intensity in Restructuring Firms: Effects of Governance, Strategy and Performance." *Academy of Management Journal,* 37 (1994): 1207–1251.

Johnson, R., R. Hoskisson, and N. Margulis. "Corporate Restructuring: Implications for Organizational Change and Development." In *Research in Organization Change and Development,* edited by W. Pasmore and R. Woodman. Greenwich: JAI Press, 1990.

Lant, T. K., and S. Mezias. "An Organizational Learning Model of Convergence and Reorientation." *Organizational Science,* 3 (1992): 47–71.

Lant, T. K., F. Milliken, and B. Batra. "The Role of Managerial Learning and Interpretation in Strategic Persistence and Reorientation: An Empirical Exploration." *Strategic Management Journal,* 13 (1992): 585–608.

Miller, D., and P. Friesen. *Organizations: A Quantum View.* Englewood Cliffs, N.J.: Prentice-Hall, 1984.

Milliken, F. J., and T. K. Lant. "The Effect of an Organization's Recent History on Strategic Persistence and Change: The Role of Managerial Interpretations." In *Advances in Strategic Management,* vol. 7, edited by J. Dutton, A. Huff, and P. Shrivastava. Greenwich, Conn.: JAI Press, 1991, pp. 125–152.

Nadler, D., R. Shaw, and A. Walton. *Discontinuous Change: Leading Organizational Transformations.* San Francisco: Jossey-Bass, 1995.

Pettigrew, A. *The Awakening Giant: Continuity and Change in Imperial Chemical Industries.* Oxford: Basil Blackwell, 1985.

Quinn, J. B. *Strategies for Change: Logical Incrementalism.* Homewood, Ill.: Irwin, 1980.

Robbins, D., and J. Pearce. "Turnaround, Retrenchment and Recovery." *Strategic Management Journal,* 13 (1992): 287–309.

Slatter, S. *Corporate Recovery: Successful Turnaround Strategies and Their Implementation.* Harmondsworth, U.K.: Penguin, 1984.

Tushman, M. L., W. H. Newman, and E. Romanelli. "Convergence and Upheaval: Managing the Unsteady Pace of Organizational Evolution." *California Management Review,* 29, no. 1 (1986): 29–44.

Tushman, M. L., and E. Romanelli. "Organizational Evolution: A Metamorphosis Model of Convergence and Reorientation." In *Research in Organizational Behavior,* edited by L. L. Cummings and B. W. Staw. Greenwich, Conn.: JAI Press, 1985, pp. 171–222.

Virany, B., M. Tushman, and E. Romanelli. "Executive Succession and Organization Outcomes in Turbulent Environments: An Organizational Learning Approach." *Organizational Science,* 3 (1992): 72–91.

Index

About the Authors

HUGH SHERMAN is Assistant Professor in the College of Business, Ohio University, where he specializes in strategic management, international business, and entrepreneurship. He has just completed a national study for the U.S. Department of Commerce investigating the impact of business incubators on local communities. Sherman has extensive executive experience in the United States and Europe and is a noted lecturer in executive development programs in Southeast Asia.

RAJESWARARAO CHAGANTI is Professor and Chair of the General and Strategic Management Department, School of Business and Management, Temple University. Executive Director of Temple's Institute of Global Management Studies, Chaganti teaches in the areas of strategic management and entrepreneurship and publishes widely in the journals of his fields. He is coauthor of *High Performance Management Strategies for Entrepreneurial Companies: Research Findings from Over 500 Firms* (Quorum, 1991).

ISBN 1-56720-087-7

90000>

9 781567 200874

HARDCOVER BAR CODE